Finding My Damascus

Michelle Andrea Williams

FINDING MY DAMASCUS

Editor: Caroline Anschutz

Cover Design by Michelle Andrea Williams
with Lynn Eggleton
Cover Photo: Photographer - James Smith
Location Cuyahoga Valley National Park
pixabay.com/en/users/jameslee-158922/

Printed in the United States of America

Some names and identifiers have been removed to protect individual privacy.

ISBN-13: 978-0999170205
ISBN-10: 0999170201

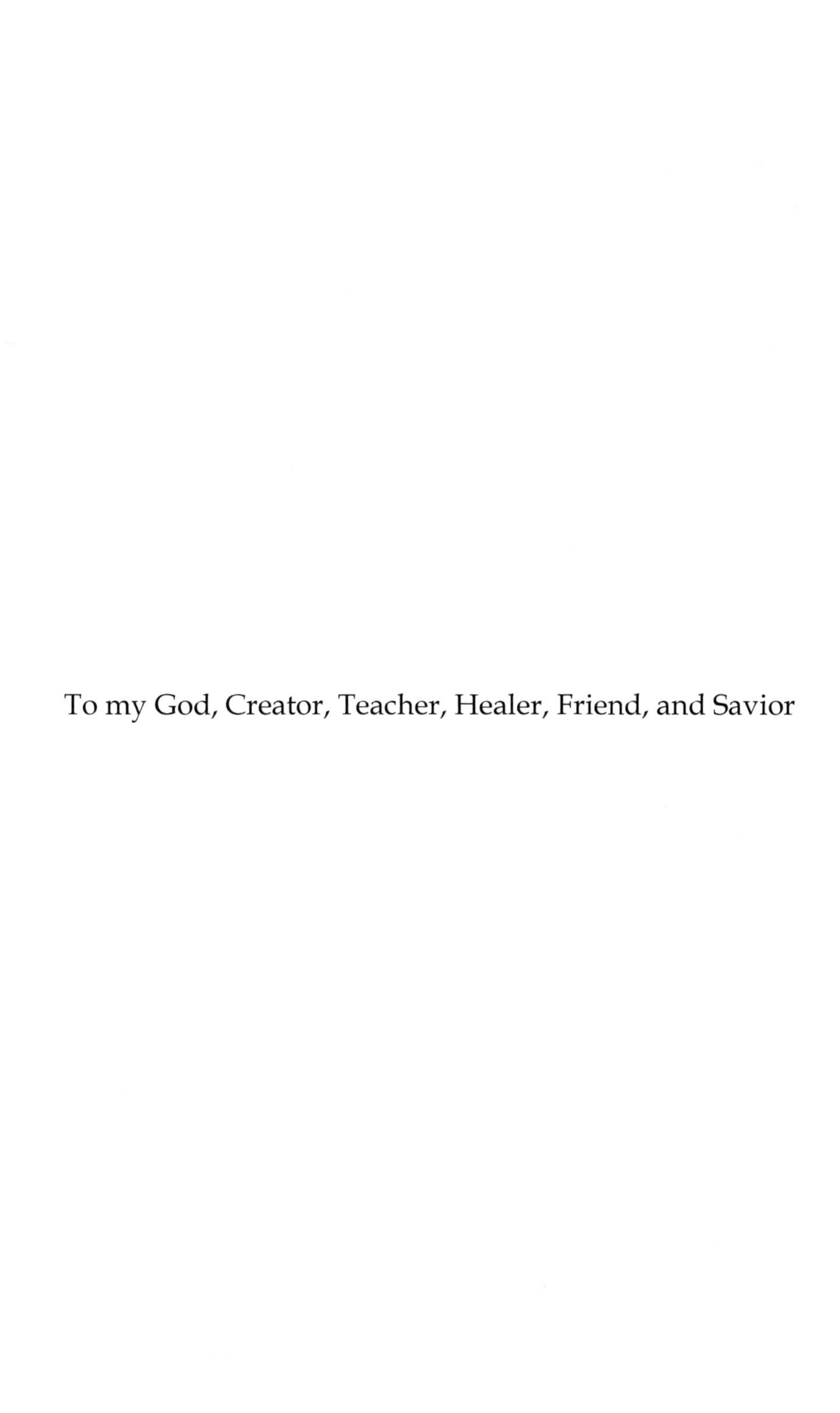

To my God, Creator, Teacher, Healer, Friend, and Savior

CONTENTS

Introduction

Damascus is a city in Syria, an ancient place appearing over fifty times in the Bible. The Bible chronicles Damascus as a way of identifying places, people, and events - war during the time of King David, a direction in the Song of Songs, and prophecies spoken against the city in Isaiah. God used this city in many ways throughout the centuries, but what Damascus is for me a place of dramatic change.

Saul was a learned scholar who studied the Law and was well versed in what God expected of him—knowledge and adherence. Others went against the Law and Saul considered them enemies of the way of life he vowed to protect. He believed the followers of Jesus were blasphemers and should be dealt with according to the Law he knew so well.

Damascus was a place in which Saul of Tarsus headed to arrest Christian men and women. Damascus was to extend Saul's reach outside Jerusalem to bring these followers of Jesus of Nazareth under control. Damascus was a mission on behalf of the authority given to Saul by the Temple. Saul had so many expectations of what would happen when he arrived. God had different plans for Damascus and for Saul.

Saul's vision of God changed after the encounter on the Road to Damascus. His transformation during the three days of blindness, fasting and isolation revealed a new-born creature, a beloved child, a believer in the Messiah. Damascus became the place God used to get Saul's undivided attention, a place in which a healing would occur, and where believers came to help.

Damascus was ground zero for Saul to become Paul, a new creature, a reborn believer, and a profoundly changed man. Damascus was not just the place of conversion, or of healing and baptism, it was the training ground for the journey to begin. Paul spent time with other Christians, preached in the Temple for the first time, and experienced condemnation for his beliefs. All he experienced in Damascus would show him the life God was leading him to live—as a follower of Jesus Christ.

The following chapters offer stories of my life before and the first several years after I became a Christian. Each story has a lesson for what God was preparing me for - a great and demanding journey. It was my training ground, a place in my life in which I needed to re-learn, examine, and contemplate my life and my choices.

God brought me to a place of self-evaluation and it was a struggle. Change is hard and difficult—I still go through massive and profound changes. Life would get no better by me doing the same things over again.

Although these lessons happened between 2010 and 2012, each remains fresh because I wrote in a journal about each one. Writing down my thoughts and feelings was great therapy and helped sort out many issues. After two years of writing, I filled three complete journals. I look back to understand the *Michelle* I used to be and the *Michelle* I have become - the one God designed.

The changes I underwent helped prepare me for the most difficult journey of my life—to be who God created me to be and to be a believer and follower of Jesus Christ.

STUDY GUIDE & JOURNAL

Each chapter holds a study guide and several pages to journal. I pray God will lead you through each question to find more of Him, of His Son, and fill you with the Holy Spirit to understand more of who He created you to be - His.

I will sprinkle clean water on you, and you will be clean; I will cleanse you from all your impurities and from all your idols. I will give you a new heart and put a new spirit in you; I will remove from you your heart of stone and give you a heart of flesh. And I will put my Spirit in you and move you to follow my decrees and be careful to keep my laws.
Ezekiel 36:25-27

Finding My Damascus

1
The Rabbit Hole

Paul's Lesson:
"What a wretched man I am! Who will rescue me from this body that is subject to death?"
Romans 7:24

The story of *Alice in Wonderland* by Lewis Carroll, in its 1972 movie adaptation, *Alice's Adventures in Wonderland,* freaked me out. The story, the characters, that Cheshire Cat and his creepy shadow smile, the chaos, all gave me great anxiety, but it was Alice who troubled me the most.

From where I sat on my couch at seven, legs tucked under, and eating an apple, Wonderland was not a wonderful place. It was a land full of insanity and confusion—where havoc wreaked. Everyone around Alice was nuts. They knew it, but didn't care. Even the Cheshire Cat said, "Everyone in Wonderland is mad, otherwise they wouldn't be down here." [1]

Were Alice's decisions born out of the madness and the unpredictable world into which she had fallen? Eat this, drink that, grow tall, shrink small. She never knew what would happen next. Was Alice's fate in the hands of others who were untrustworthy, always changing, and selfish? Did she have any control at all? She was the one who had fallen down the rabbit hole–down the long dark tunnel, falling, falling until she hit bottom into the insanity.

The summer before my sophomore year in high school, I went on a two-week vacation with extended family. I knew the relatives my entire life, but spent little time with them without my parents. One of the male relatives sexually molested me over this two-week period. It was subtle at first, a touch here, a brush there, which could have seemed innocent. Then it built up to a clear, repulsive violation. I ripped apart at the seams. My safety, security, and sanity—gone.

I reported it to my family and was on a flight home the next day. round of *I'm sorry that happened* and *What do you need?* but then nothing. No charges filed, no counseling, not much talking after the event—silence. Like it never happened, but it did.

My actions and decisions became foreign, haphazard, and compulsive. I would head away from the safety of my home looking for situations that were unhealthy and dangerous. I became a victim again and again. Each encounter painted the undeserving, worthless self-image I framed. This lasted the rest of the summer.

Feelings of anguish and filth prompted me to bathe often to rid the dirtiness enveloping me. At midnight, 3am, 2 o'clock in the afternoon, looking for a way to wash it all away and disappear. It didn't work. Clear signs of trauma, but no one noticed.

Before the following school year, I turned to alcohol and marijuana for escape. It was as unnatural as Alice eating a piece of the mushroom or drinking the tiny bottles of potion, but I didn't care. I wanted the pain, humiliation, and shame to vanish. The pain pushed down just below the surface of my skin, and I became numb to it—for a while.

During a heavy period of smoking marijuana, close to the end of my sophomore year, I realized how much the dope was affecting my brain. Memories of when I was high were crystal clear while memories when sober were smoky and worn. I quit in that moment. I no longer wanted stonewashed memories, but there was a catch—unworthiness and depression resurfaced

My junior and senior years of high school were better and I dated a young man for the next three years. I became productive and involved myself in many activities, including the debate team, chess club, photography, yearbook, and baseball statistician. But my personal relationships were unhealthy and dependent.

By the time I reached college, I fell deeper into the rabbit hole. Making it through my freshman year, I suffered from severe depression during the sophomore year. Ditching classes, missing work study, overeating, oversleeping and falling so much farther down the rabbit hole, it was not a surprise I flunked out on an academic suspension. After which, I moved back home with my parents.

That summer, my core came unraveled. I had a waitressing job about 20 miles from my parent's house. The drives to and from work, my mind filled with battle plans. I was fighting for relief, still suffering, still broken, I wanted out. How was I to end this? Thoughts defaulted to planning my suicide—picking a large tree, foot to the floor, turning the wheel and bam! Done. It would be done.

I was so damaged. I ended the relationship with my high school boyfriend. I was searching for answers, relief, distraction, even a savior, but I found all the wrong things through a married, alcoholic, older man. I abandoned my job, my family, friends, home, any convictions I had left - everything to be with him. He became the god in my life, took over all I was and controlled my existence.

Six months into the adulterous relationship and a secret move to Florida, I was pregnant. I moved back home, keeping the baby a secret from my family. My parents set up a cot in the living room for me to sleep. I had betrayed them with lies and manipulation, the cot was all I deserved. But I still didn't disclose my pregnancy until, by accident, I spoke of it to a friend on the phone and my youngest sister overheard.

So where was the father? Why was I not with him? He went back to his wife several times, but we continued to see each other. He gave me a set of bridal rings to show he promised, someday, after his divorce to marry me. I held on to the promise believing all would be well.

When I was four months pregnant, we moved in together—after his wife kicked him out. We lived in a trailer, one of several we would live in together. We moved often from one trailer park to another, then a rental house, then another trailer. I felt grateful to have a roof over my head and a warm place to sleep.

Under each roof, there were growing problems filled with addiction, authoritarianism, verbal abuse, fighting, crying, a blanket of darkness. I thought, *maybe he will change after we have the baby. Maybe he will treat me with respect because I gave up everything for him.* I was fooling myself.

Thoughts of suicide diminished as my belly grew with this baby. I was no longer planning to end my life and yet held deep anxiety over staying alive. I had to care for this precious child. The chaotic circumstances had not changed, the situation was the same, but this baby changed my thinking. I valued my life again.

NOTE: *God led me to interject at this point and discuss my pregnancy. Although the thoughts of suicide dissipated while I was pregnant, my unhealthy choices and brokenness continued. I carried these into motherhood. Pregnancy was not my cure for what was wrong. Therapy and profound healing would have been God's plan for me and I didn't see it until much later in life.*

Dark and smoky, smelling of decades of spilled alcohol and nicotine, I sat at the end of the bar. Seven months pregnant in white maternity shorts and extra-large pink tank-top, I chatted with the lady bartender while she served beer after beer to patrons. I wore the *promise* wedding ring and drank a Coke.

He sat perpendicular on the long end of the bar as if we were at a small bistro table. Cigarette in one hand, beer in the other, deep in a drunk, each glass made his eyes a little more glazed. I watched him and pretended to be his wife with the pawn shop rings on my finger. *Close enough,* I thought, *I was his girlfriend and was carrying his child—doesn't that count for something?*

A tall, blonde-haired woman walked by and I saw it - this myth I was conjuring up, this self-deceit, *this* lie. As she passed, he turned around—not just his head but his whole body -and gave a direct, lust-filled look. As their eyes met, my soul ripped apart. My heart crushed, my eyes filled with fiery tears, my throat collapsed—fury and pain erupted.

"I am sitting right HERE," I cried through his drunkenness. "Right here, carrying YOUR child, and you are looking at another woman? Right in front of me? Don't I even matter? Don't I exist?"

These same words likely said by his wife while we were dating. How foolish I was, how ignorant and unhealthy, to think taking part in an affair was more acceptable than being the one betrayed. How could I be so irrational to think the same man who cheated on his own wife, with me, would then have the heart and mind to be faithful? Insane!

From that moment on, I accepted the relationship as it was - unfaithful, miserable, damaged, and deserved. I gave birth to my son a few months later. I was a mother and I loved my baby boy. He slept well at night and rarely cried. As he grew into a toddler and then a preschooler, the toxic relationship with the father continued. We married several years later, yet the relationship deteriorated. When my son started kindergarten, I got a job, bought a car, secured a place to live, and left the marriage. I was a single mother. Marriage number one was over and I was still broken.

Within months, I dated again. Soon, I dated a man who would be in my life for the next eleven years. The relationship was one-sided. I was the one who made most of the effort—the phone calls, the trips over to the other side of the county, and arrangements for the vacations. Each Saturday night, I went to his house and woke up on Sunday to cook breakfast. Sunday afternoon, we watched sports, and later I traveled home.

Three years into the relationship, he had yet to say he loved me. I broke the relationship off and dated someone else for a few months. Six months later, we reconciled and, although he said he loved me, we slipped back into the weekly routine for another eight years. It went on and on.

I became the enabler for a man who seldom worked and spent most of his money on alcohol. I had a relationship of co-dependency and continued to wait for him to change. It never happened.

Brokenness settled into my bones and became part of my normalcy. By my late twenties and throughout my thirties, I was a self-proclaimed pagan, studying and practicing wiccan and natural spirituality. Never practicing in a group, I kept this secret to myself and it from my family. I thought it would change my life and give me control, a new direction, and a reliance. I believed I could summon spirits to do my bidding and have all I dreamed and desired.

During those years, I dismissed the ideology of a Trinity, of a Savior, the Holy Spirit, and One Creator above all else. I called on *other entities* to help me and use pagan practices to bend the universe to my will—this was my belief.

The spells and incantations reflected my self-centeredness. I called on spirits to aid me in changing a situation, a relationship, the future, all the while invoking something other than my Creator. So, what was it I was entertaining in my spiritual practice? Anything and everything not of God.

I did several positive things in my life around this time like going back to college and earning my bachelor's degree; purchasing a fixer upper home in a nice neighborhood; and continued to raise my son the best way I knew as a single parent.

I came across a book during this time which guided me to heal from the trauma I suffered in my teens. *The Courage to Heal: A Guide for Women Survivors of Child Sexual Abuse* by Ellen Bass and Laura Davis. I worked on this diligently, wrote letters to my abuser, and came to a place of understanding, if not complete healing. The activities in the book allowed me to gain courage to discuss and resolve some of my issues, but there was much more left undone.

The answers to all my remaining problems, I thought, were in the pagan practices - but there was a price to pay. Entities I invited to join me, I believed, stayed in my home and influenced the atmosphere. Whenever there was depression, anger, conflict or fear, it was as if a congressional assembly descended on the house to amplify the atmosphere.

In my late thirties, I met the man who became my second husband. We worked for the same company. Friends at first, but when he got separated from his first wife, I ended my eleven-year relationship, and we started dating. A few months later, he moved in. A year later we married—too fast, too soon and for the wrong reasons.

Soon after we married, I stopped the pagan practices. By the second year of marriage, after reconciling from a four-month separation, we were attending a local church with our friends, Will and Darlene. Church was sanctuary for me during the two-hour service and I rested in the peace and comfort

I believe the residual effects of my pagan practices fed the flames of chaos. Situations that would have dissipated instead escalated to hellish levels. What would start as a simple disagreement between me and my second spouse became hours of debate and arguing. The situation would morph into a hole punched in the wall or a broken appliance. The atmosphere in our home became unbearable. I felt there was a spiritual battle building to a final showdown.

The marriage deteriorated and I was still broken. The financial situation with job layoffs and overspending led to bankruptcy. Alcohol abuse was a contributing factor. Something needed to change and it wasn't happening where and how we were living.

After almost four years of marriage, he moved out of state back with his parents. The plan was for me to join him after I found a job and sold the house. I made trips every couple of weeks to see him and expected I would get a job interview at any moment. It never happened. I applied for 313 jobs and nothing materialized.

In the meantime, I was alone. My son was grown and married. I went to work and came home to an empty house. The depression consumed me once again. Sitting in darkness each evening, depression embraced me. I was falling down the rabbit hole once more, but this time I had a life line to grab hold of each Sunday.

I felt a sense of safety in attending church and being around believers who were encouraging and supportive. The love I felt from others chipped away at the thick wall I constructed over the decades. They showed love without judgement or condemnation. I no longer wanted to deny God or ignore Him.

Several months after my spouse moved, there a moment in which I realized my second marriage was over. A phone call one night confirmed my spouse's plans did not include me. I was an afterthought and no longer mattered. Our marriage didn't matter and the financial recovery from bankruptcy was not on the radar. I ended the marriage and we separated for the final time.

The twenty plus years of bad life decisions caught up with me. Depressed and desperate for healing, I wanted out of the rabbit hole. Exhausted and bankrupt, I was furious with my choices, my unhealthiness, and my ungodly ways of living. How could I have let this insanity take me floundering through life? How could I have thought my will power was enough to have complete healing, happiness, wholeness and peace?

I sat on the floor of my soon-to-be-foreclosed home, not knowing what would happen next. I was at the bottom of my brokenness and in my darkest hour. In the middle of those crushing circumstances pinning me to the floor, I was ready to find God.

I sobbed, "I am tired of living like this. I screwed up my life and stink at making my own decisions. I am ready to live Your Way. Take over my life and do what You need to do with me. I AM ALL YOURS."

Only then could my crying out begin.

Road Signs

In Michelle's first steps, she discovered her ways and decisions were not healthy. She could not make the necessary changes on her own and needed God's help. God was always there, even when she refused to acknowledge Him. God patiently waited for her to hit the lowest point and find Him.

Think of a time when you thought God was absent from your life:

What events or life situations were happening during this time?

How did you feel?

Looking back, what moment could you point to in which you now see God was there?

What steps can you take now to invite more of God's presence into your life?

I am set apart with the dead,
like the slain who lie in the grave,
whom you remember no more,
who are cut off from your care.
You have put me in the lowest pit,
in the darkest depths.
Psalm 88:5-7

Journal:

____

____

____

____

____

____

2
Crying Out

Paul's Lesson:

"'What shall I do, Lord?' I asked.
"'Get up,' the Lord said, 'and go into Damascus. There you will be told all that you have been assigned to do.'"
Acts 22:10

The events of the last few decades overwhelmed me. I felt as if pieces of myself scattered along the way and I had little skill to gather each again. Anxiety and panic attacks once again as I became immersed in the grief over my second marriage ending.

So much hurt needed healing. Where was I to begin? How did all this work? I spent the first month crying uncontrollably. I woke up each day feeling like I was drowning and had to fight for air to keep breathing. And life didn't stop.

I started a new role at work and during my training with a co-worker, I wept. Preparing for my upcoming MBA graduation, my excitement in reaching this milestone waned. The decision to sign my house over to the bankruptcy court should have been heartbreaking; I felt relief instead.

I rented a one-bedroom apartment in Petersburg, Virginia, one town over from my home of ten years. After paying a hefty deposit for bad credit, I had a quiet place of my own. My new home became a sanctuary for recovery and healing.

I talked with friends and sought advice to help lift my emotions to higher ground. Each Sunday, I heard positive sermons both convicting and biblical. On Wednesday nights, I attended Bible study and searched God's Word for answers. I even purchased self-help talks to ease my anxiety and sadness. And I prayed – a lot.

I understood God in three parts - Father, Son-Christ, and Holy Spirit. Logically, we are created in His image and can be viewed in three parts. The body—the biological temple to house the spirit; the mind—the consciousness and brain which influences us; and the spirit—the true self requires attention and nurturing. I had neglected all three.

I needed an action plan to put the lost and broken pieces back together. For the body, I walked and worked out. My mind needed new focus and learn something new, so I found and put a deposit on a Latin dance class starting in two months. The list of action items helped, but I was trying to fill my life with answers without understanding the questions. I needed more.

I went to the local book store and bought a new Bible, a New International Version, leather bound and beautiful. I had other Bibles, but this one was special. I bought it as an investment into the new relationship I requested just a few weeks prior. Then, I found and scheduled an appointment with a therapist.

The first visit was about a month after I separated from spouse number two in April 2010. Her office was an old renovated wayside hotel, the ones you see all along the old byways abandoned after the main highways were built. The re-purposed hotel efficiencies became craft shops, hair salons, and business offices.

One of those former efficiencies was transformed into a cozy therapy office. What used to be a living room, kitchen, and bedroom, were now the waiting area, office and therapy area. Overstuffed couches and chairs with soft-lit lamps and pretty curtains made me feel I was visiting someone's tiny home. I felt comfortable.

She had dark hair, a round face, and little over five feet tall. Her demeanor was one of an acquaintance wanting to get to know me better, but not disclosing herself too much. She had a genuine interest in understanding who I was, but a necessary wall built as was proper for her profession. She was like the eccentric aunt who would listen for hours, yet you barely knew who she was.

Our first session began. I settled into the couch that left my feet dangling. She took a seat in a winged back chair; her legs folded under and hands balancing a yellow legal pad and pen. I was ready to unlock, to look inside, to see what would appear in the mirror in front of me, and talk through all this mess. I was not prepared for what came out.

She asked open ended questions - why I was there that day, what did I expect from our sessions, how was I feeling in that moment. I took a deep breath and used it to unload the separation, the loss, the pain, the most recent long list of failures. She allowed me to talk it out and she scribbled unknown words.

Then, time was up. It seemed abrupt and cold. I didn't know if I felt any better or worse. I left with little hope, defeated, unresolved; but I came back. Another session came and went—same method of questions and answers and I felt little different, *maybe*. Was this even working?

Several sessions later, I rehashed the same old stuff. How many times could I talk about the betrayal, the hurt, the sorrow? How was this going to change anything? I was getting frustrated. This was doing no good. I was wasting my time. Then she hit me with a brick of a question.

"Why are you overly responsible for everyone else?" she asked.

What? I thought, *Overly responsible? What is she asking? I am not overly responsible! She has some nerve!*

I sat there stunned. Our session was over, she had saved the throwing of the brick for last. My face flushed with embarrassment and surprise, I left furious, betrayed, hurt—all from one question.

I mulled it over in my mind. I turned it over and around to look at it from different angles. She didn't ask me *if* I was overly responsible, or *did I think* I was—she asked *why are you*. She showed me a truth and asked for an explanation, like a child caught coloring with crayons on the wall. Not blaming the child but acknowledging the resulting mess and working to discover what possessed the child to do such a thing.

Two weeks passed to allow me to unravel the question she asked of me. I began - I was helpful, supportive, courteous, respectful, but overly responsible? *Why* was I doing the helpful things I did? Was it because someone needed me? Could they not do those things for themselves? What was I getting out of it? What was the purpose?

Responsible[2] is defined as an obligation to do something, to have control over, or to care for someone. It also means being the primary cause of something to be blamed or credited for it.

Overly[3] means excessively. The root question was "Why was I excessively obligated, controlling, and caring for others?"

Controlling and obligated? Was it caring? Was I a controlling person? Had I, through the years, been *un*caring in my actions? By the time the next session rolled around, I was still bothered but not as incensed as our last parting. I saw a lifetime of patterns in the question. Doing for and helping others *excessively* took the focus from doing for and helping myself. It was not genuine caring, but an act of selfish, false fulfillment. Quite a painful revelation.

My therapist greeted me with the kind smile she always displayed. Her no-nonsense approach was comforting. I sat on the couch across from the winged back chair, her legs tucked once more with notebook on her lap, and pen ready to wield new notes. She stared at me for a moment with her and said, "I pissed you off last time, didn't I?"

My eyes widened. Startled, I replied, "Yes! Yeah, you did. You said I was *overly responsible*."

She explained, "I don't sit around saying, 'Oh let me see what I can say to make Michelle mad today.' I waited until the moment was right for you to look inside and understand something about yourself. All I am doing is what you hired me to do. Help you. That's what you pay me to do."

The one question flipped a switch in my brain. The mirror was in front of me. Was it insensible to help a person out by buying a few groceries though all their money used to buy liquor? Offer someone a place to live because they could not afford a place on their own? Give love when it wasn't returned in a way in which I felt loved? Take a partner back after infidelity? Overlook another's faults even when the shortcomings were potentially dangerous? Be responsible for each relationship and expect *nothing* in return? Wrong. I was wrong.

What she did worked. For the first time, I looked at my behavior, my choices, my thoughts, my actions, and aspects of myself I had not noticed. She did her job. She helped me see myself, without judgement, without guilt—viewing those things I refused to see on my own.

After more sessions, we would unravel bits and pieces I needed to look at and ponder. What I did with those realizations was my responsibility and my choice. She was there to guide me, a psychological reference book to help me understand my next steps in healing.

In one of the last sessions, through another round of sobbing, my counselor observed, "You know when you cry the hardest? When you talk about your marriage ending, not about your spouse being out of your life."

I said, "Do I? I didn't realize it."

She asked, "Why do you think that is?"

I thought for a moment and the realization surprised me, "I cry when I talk about my marriage ending because…I feel like I have failed God." She sat back in the winged back chair and smiled.

I desired to please God now, to come to know Him and understand what He wanted from me. I wanted to be perfect and never be a disappointment. How could I believe I managed God's affection for me? That I controlled whether He loved me or turned from me? I was being *overly responsible*—for God's relationship with me!

I found I didn't know God at all. My version was one of the all-powerful Father sitting on the thrown judging whether I was good enough to draw his attention. Since I knew I was bad, broken, unworthy, why bother? Why not try something else? I would never be good enough to earn His love, much less a glance in my direction.

When I came back to church, it differed from the Methodist Church in which I grew up attending. The sermons were of Love, Acceptance, Grace and Peace. Pastors used the "J" word, a litmus test I would come to give each church I entered going forward. Does the clergy say "Jesus"?

This was a new way of seeing Him, and the precipice of finding who God truly was. I longed to know this new version of God. I had been treating God like a person in one of my relationships. Never showing them the real Michelle, but the Michelle I thought they wanted to be with to secure the bond.

Fake is hard to support. If I had been faking who I was to please others for decades, then who was I? Who was Michelle? I longed to know. It became a quest, but I had much work to do. The therapy, the church services, the studying, discussions with friends, it all was leading up to change.

At three o'clock in the morning on May 26th, I woke up alone in my new apartment. My friends helped me move in and I had lived there for two months. It was the first time in my life I lived alone. It was a new experience and a new beginning.

The pastors' sermons at church, and testimony from others, introduced me to the Holy Spirit. It was the helper sent to believers to guide us and be an advocate between us and God. This was new, God speaking to me. I had never experienced it and had my doubts. It was intriguing. If it were true, I had gentle fears of what exactly God would say after my decades of living without Him.

I sleep deeply, nothing wakes me except for a child's cry in the night or a need to use the bathroom. That morning was no different, but something jarred my sleep. As I woke, I had a deep thought covering me. I don't know how else to explain this to those who have never experienced it. It was a thought not my own, a deep-seeded thought enveloping me.

"Go get your Grandfather's Bible."

A simple sentence, a request, no, a gentle command—one that would not have come from me in the wee hours of the morning. I had the other Bible, the one I had purchased for myself a few weeks prior, but God did not tell me to get that Bible. My grandfather's Bible would play the role in what unfolded.

In the 1960's and 1970's, Granddad was a technical writer for the U.S. Army during the week and a Wesleyan pastor on the weekends. He was a remarkable man - soft spoken, white-haired, intelligent, and loved to eat steak and go fishing. He was my champion, encourager, and reminder—I could be anything.

The Bible was the only personal possession I received after his death in 1990. It was leather bound, hunter green, and an early 1970's Amplified Version. His notes were written throughout and several sermons outlined on the back pages.

I climbed out of bed, walked to the living room and found my Grandfather's Bible laying on the antique buffet. Grabbing it, I made my way back to the bedroom. Turning on my nightstand lamp, I climbed back into bed. Sitting there for a moment, I let the sleep lift from my eyes and adjust to the light.

God led me to read each scripture and the thoughts came as I followed.

O sinful child, come home, for I am your master and husband. I will bring you together again from scattered pieces wherever they are and make you whole. (Jeremiah 3:14)

How long will you go back and forth, forever conforming to others version of you, daughter of mine? I will make you new and different when you come to me. (Jeremiah 33:22)

Don't mind My correction for it is not within your power that these changes will occur, but of Mine alone. I will be your Guide through it all. (Jeremiah 10:23-24)

Your past is no more, don't be afraid of it. Your shame will not define who you are, for I am your Husband, I am your God, I am your Redeemer. (Isaiah 54:4-5)

I cried out to Him and He answered me. Amid my lowest low and my pain, in my struggle to know Him. I heard the Love, the Grace, the Forgiveness, the Redemption. I found Him. All the tears of shame, the lies, the hurt, all came out that morning and in many mornings and nights to come.

This was ground zero for the work laid before me. It was my Damascus – the place in which God had my undivided attention, to discover who I truly was, and who God created me to be. I wanted to know more of Him – this Creator who took the time to show me He had a plan, He loved me immensely right where I was, and would partner with me in the journey ahead.

How He Loves by David Crowder Band resonated with me during this time of crying out. As our church choir sang its own rendition, God's words of Love filled my heart. This was the beginning. God loved me right where I was and He would not leave me there. He had a plan.

Soon after, my classes started and I learned to dance.

Road Signs

In Michelle's second part of the journey, she realized her own actions were the ones leading to her situation. She sought professional help during this time of grief and depression. Michelle also realized God's love for her was unconditional and she was not in control of it. She could do nothing to make God either love her or reject her - His love is constant.

Think of a time when you went through a traumatic situation:

How did you manage the grief or stress in your life?

What help did you seek for those tough, dark moments?

What would you say to God about your experience during this time?

How would you expect God to answer you if you asked Him for help?

As for me, I call to God,
and the Lord saves me.
Evening, morning and noon
I cry out in distress,
and he hears my voice.
Psalm 55:16-18

Journal:

3
The Dance

Paul's Lesson:
For those who are led by the Spirit of God are the children of God.
Romans 8:14

I was never a great dancer and was told so by someone I dated. Harsh, but true. I am not coordinated and the control of muscle movement is not one of my genetic talents. But I love music and, from the release of Saturday Night Fever in the 1970s onward, always wanted to dance. However, my wish to dance and my ability were on opposite sides of the spectrum.

In June 2010, I took dance lessons from a reputable dance studio led by a husband and wife team. It was a little pricey, but worth it to have professional dance instructors. The dance lessons I chose were Latin. I enjoyed Latin music, especially Carlos Santana and the many accompanying artists belting out his heartbeat through song and sound.

The dance studio was above a Mexican restaurant and bar, and the wooden stairs and dance floor creaked with age. I showed up with newly purchased dance shoes - slight heel and quite comfortable. As I entered the studio, I saw a beautiful, slender lady with years of dancing showing through her stature and walk. I knew nothing of choreographed or classic dance moves, but anyone could tell she knew her craft well—even standing still.

This was Salsa 101, a beginner's class and one you could take with or without a partner. Other class members were excited to learn. The first few lessons were learning our steps—one set for the ladies and another for the men.

She showed the female's steps first, then she switched and showed the male's steps. Each step and arm position, both male and female, were a mirror image of the another. Each student was expected to learn their designated movements before learning to dance as partners. I watched her feet move in rhythm with the Latin beat moving in specific patterns across the dance studio floor. I listened and watched with earnest, hoping to transfer the talent to my own muscles.

Watching someone dance and then mimicking the form were completely out of my domain. My feet were like dead weights with no wish to be in rhythm or in sequence to the pattern. I moved, my feet in off-beat, awkward placement. I kept moving. Step after step, getting the sequence right then wrong, then wrong again. The teacher offered the only advice that would help me—practice—a lot!

I felt defeated and inadequate like I was stuck in the rabbit hole, but still determined to learn to dance. Inside the building where I worked, there was a fitness center with its own dance studio. Here is where I practiced. I could not rely on my sight to make sure my feet moved the right way. I had to *feel* I was moving in the right direction, keeping balanced Eyes closed, headphones in, proper Santana song thumping the rhythm, I forced my feet into the memorized design. My feet felt each movement and hit the marks until I opened my eyes, then my steps would falter.

After two introductory lessons and hours of practice, I began to master my own steps and it felt quite natural. My muscles remembered the movements and complied when requested. I gained confidence and felt more comfortable with my abilities.

Dancing alone is unique. I controlled the steps, the movement, the timing, but it took a partner to experience the fullness of the dance. The third lesson was about learning to put my dance moves into a partnership - a mirrored pairing. Knowing my own steps allowed me to try the next level - a fluid syncing with a partner.

My partner was an older gentleman, Latino, and devoted to learning the Salsa. I could tell from the earlier lesson, he had practiced as much as I did, and probably more. As we stood face to face, the teacher advised us of the proper hold, hands clasped firm but fluid, the correct foot poised to begin the sequence of steps, I was ready, or so I thought.

The music began. The class members, now knowing their own steps, danced together. I took a step, then two, then another and felt like all the practice had worked, then I tried to move in a direction I was not supposed to go. My partner pulled as I pushed, then pushed as I pulled. He stopped, frowning with furrowed brow as if scolding me. We reset our stance and began again.

This time we got further into the sequence of movements, but again, I pushed and he pulled, then I pulled and he pushed. What was going on here? What was happening? I thought I was taking the right foot position, body position for the female, but something was amiss.

In his lovely accent, he explained "You are not letting me lead."

"Oh, the man is supposed to lead?" I blurted out.

"Yes, just let me lead. You'll see," he invited.

I thought it was a partnership in which I did my steps, he did his, and the combined dance would become one motion. No one told me the man *leads* while all of this is going on. I tried again and surrendered my movement so he could lead me through the steps. My steps were patterned and purposeful, but he led the dance.

We tried again. I relaxed, he led, I followed, and we danced. My muscles were conditioned to think for themselves and it would take purposeful relaxation to allow another to lead me on the dance floor. More starts and stops, more practice, he smiled an assurance I was complying with his earlier request.

My feet felt surer, my arms locked in position and held strong, and I was feeling my part with total understanding of his role. Dancing with someone else was a partnership, a trust, and a full cooperation. But I had more to learn, much more.

The studio held a dance party once a month open to the public. Those that went, the teachers explained, wanted to show their moves and practice, nothing more. After two months of dance lessons, I decided to attend. I wore a nice dress, short sleeves, lots of deodorant, and my dance shoes.

I walked into the studio and it was transformed into a dance party with chair lining the walls, Christmas lights flashing, a DJ, and about a hundred people mingling about. Men and women, all ranges of skill levels and ages.

An older gentleman approached within minutes of my arrival and asked me to dance the Rumba. "I don't know how," I confessed loudly over the Latin beat, "I never learned the Rumba."

"That's ok, come on, I'll lead. It'll be fun," he assured me. He led off and I clumsily followed trying to keep in step and mirror his movements. Logically, like Salsa, the female steps complimented the male, but I didn't know the pattern.

Now, I understand the Rumba starts with a basic box step and then spins and turns are added to make it fun and fancy. That night, whether he thought it humorous or was simply trying to enjoy himself, he added those fancy turns. I was like a Raggedy Ann doll trailing behind. It was a mess and I didn't enjoy getting swung around across the crowded dance floor.

When the song finished, I was exhausted. He thanked me for dancing and encouraged me to practice my moves. I found a perimeter chair to catch my breath and watched the next dance and then the next. There were ladies with beautiful, flowing moves and others even more uncoordinated than me. And there were men who were so graceful and skilled that the ladies, whether they were great dancers or not, vied for their attention.

One dancer was popular. He was in our advanced dance class, about 30 years old, and terrific dancer with a smile and personality to match. He was not there to pick up women, but loved dancing with each one. Later in the evening, after I danced with a few inexperienced participants, he asked me to dance. It was a Salsa and I felt comfortable I would dance well.

He led off and I followed, my feet tapping each step to the beat. I was enjoying myself when he said, "Um, you look like you're squashing bugs with your feet."

I felt my face rise to inflamed. "What do you mean?" I asked indignantly.

How could he think I wasn't doing a good job with my footwork? I knew the right steps, I was following his lead, what more what there? How dare he criticize my dancing! Didn't he know how bad I *used* to be?

He laughed to ease my grave scowl and explained, "When you place your foot on the floor, so forceful you look like you are trying to kill a spider. You need to learn to trust the floor, trust your movements. The floor is your friend, not your enemy. Use it as part of the dance."

I was so adamant about the proper placement of my feet I lost sight of how the steps were supposed to flow, and how the floor provides the platform to glide, twirl, and move. I felt like a four-year-old girl in ballet class, knowing the right steps, but not having the technique or experience to execute each gracefully.

As I was rethinking the floor and its purpose, the young man asked me to dance again. He didn't intend to leave me with those thoughts without helping me discover their use. I relaxed, he led, I followed and imagined my feet barely touching the floor, just skimming it as we moved across the room like a knife spreading sweet icing. I felt foolish for reacting as I did and now knowing he was only helping me and I thanked him for his insight.

"Practice," he said, "That time was better. You'll get the hang of it." And I knew I would.

I thought I had the skills to be a good partner. My ego led me to believe I was the one who had it together and my partners were the ones who didn't know how to *dance.* After two failed marriages, and a failed long-term relationship, the only constant factor in those situations was me. I was the partner who didn't know my steps.

I needed to learn new skills, a new way of thinking, God's way about life, love, and relationships. God taught me through this dance class I needed to learn to first *dance* with God before partnering with anyone else. I needed His expertise to learn these skills.

But, knowing the right skills is only part of it. I had to let God lead me. I also had to *trust the floor,* the foundation God was building under my life, the safety net to hold me. Only He could guide me in the right direction, signal a turn, create momentum, and equalize tension to make a fluid and beautiful experience.

Whatever You're Doing (Something Heavenly) by Sanctus Real showed me *I wanted God to guide me, lead me to do His will* (Psalm 143:10). I needed to evaluate, release, and be open to instruction. God was changing me which were new and different - of thinking and being. I was gaining a clear picture of His methods and how He was guiding me to transform.

Just as in the dance lessons, I had to listen to God's instructions, heed His advice, and make the necessary changes. But first, I had to agree to submit myself and surrender to His ways.

Road Signs

Michelle's third lesson was about allowing God to lead and order her steps. She had to learn to relinquish control and let God show her His ways. Michelle also understood she didn't know how to be a good partner in life and there was much work to do to remedy decades of bad decisions.

Recall a moment in your life when you felt like a situation was out of your control:

What role did the other people play in the situation?

What hurts did you or someone suffer during this time?

When looking back, what would you have done another way?

What do you think God would have wanted you to do in a different way?

What lesson can you gather from this situation to allow you to be a healthier person?

Send me your light and your faithful care,
let them lead me;
let them bring me to your holy mountain,
to the place where you dwell.
Psalm 43:3

Journal:

4
Surrender

Paul's Lesson:
The mind governed by the flesh is death, but the mind governed by the Spirit is life and peace.
Romans 8:6

A touchy word, surrender, for one used to doing things her own way—all the time. Resisting or opposing is the reverse of surrendering. You would think my dance lesson would readjust my attitude and make me think different. I understood the concept, I had a bad, bad habit going on.

A simple phrase that rarely left my mouth or even entered my brain was, *I don't know*. Since I knew everything there was to know, even when I didn't, I pretended to show the world and myself I was in control. To think I knew the answer to everything made me arrogant, prideful, and self-righteous.

This part of my personality did not leave just because I had an encounter with God, understood the lessons of the dance, and went to church twice a week. I had many changes to make and a lot of maturing to do.

Three months into my separation, several things happened. First, I graduated with my MBA. Yay, positive! I had completed my studies despite the crying, separation, moving, and chaos. I attended graduation in Washington, DC and several members of my family were there.

Second, I traveled quite a bit for work, which was another positive. I enjoyed the training I led for people and going to new and different places. I spent most of the summer in east Texas at a warehouse startup and became friends with some of the staff. Miss Penny, Stuart, and others were beautiful people who encouraged me during this time.

Third, I started dating someone in June of 2010, several months before my divorce was legal in September. This was contrary to the commitment I made to myself not to date until the divorce was final. I let myself down once again.

When I first met this gentleman, I advised him not to call me until after the divorce. I gave him a brief but thorough history of my life and its failures. Two weeks after we met, he called. He had not listened and decided not to wait. I dismissed it and agreed to go out. This was one of many red flags during the six months to follow showing me he did not have my best interests at heart.

Even after all I had been through with three failed relationships, I jumped into a relationship with a man who displayed the same worrying characteristics. And I fell back into being a version of Michelle that would appease him and keep him interested.

The only thing different this go around was God. Through this time, God showed me how a person who seems nice, kind, intelligent, and caring can also be self-centered, controlling, and opportunistic. And the biggest issue was no spirituality. I saw no relationship with God and no wish to seek God in any way.

One of his friends, Stevie, was a believer. He was a man who struggled with life, but had a relationship with God. Stevie and I had many conversations and shared stories of God's intervention in our lives. One evening, as all three of us were heading out to hear a band, Stevie turned to his friend said, "You are taking her away from God."

The more time I spent with this man, the more distant I felt from God. My feelings of shame, emptiness, and depression returned. What was I doing? Was this another lesson I had to learn or the same one repeating itself? How was I missing God in all of this? Was this man going to drastically change into someone who God wanted me to partner?

I was lost again. How could I let this happen? *Boy, do I stink at this, Lord.* I complied with what others expected of me, to be the person they wanted me to be—but it was a lie. If this man saw me as I truly was, would he be interested? Probably not.

I disconnected from him, rarely calling, and let the relationship take its natural waning course. This was difficult for me, someone who valued what others thought and conformed to the image others expected. When this did not happen, anxiety filled me to overflowing.

After two months of little effort from me, I suspected he began dating someone else. I had the ache from childhood of always wanting to be valued, to be wanted by someone I cared for, and when it was not reciprocated, panic.

I was at my sister's house for a visit one evening and had a powerful anxiety attack—feelings of unworthiness, loneliness, and betrayal. These were familiar. Such feelings would drape heavily and pin me to the floor. My breathing became shallow, my heart pounded deep and loud, my throat closed. I had to leave. I told my sister goodbye and drove away.

Through the dark, back roads, I headed home on the 30-minute drive. During the anxiety attack, I prayed—hard! It drained my energy and left me in a puddle of muck, exhausted. I did not want this anymore, this self-defeat, this pitiful shame. For the first time, I realized I didn't deserve to feel this way. I deserved more and only God could help me. Again, I cried out, "God take this mess. I give it all to you."

A moment of true surrender. Through tears and sobbing, I handed it over to Him, all of it. I asked God to enter the depths of my heart, my torn little heart, my mind, full of fear and torment, and my spirit, broken and struggling, and heal me. This was a different request from the first time. I had asked God to take over my life, all of it, I was all His. I had opened the door. This time, I invited Him inside.

The next moments changed me forever. I let go and He jumped in to lead the dance. Love, Warmth, and Happiness flooded me. My crying change to laughter—out loud! I was deeply, whole-heartedly, joyfully laughing. My heart filled full of Love and Joy. This was like nothing I had ever experienced. In that moment, God healed me from wanting approval from others, from debilitating anxiety attacks, from believing the lies of unworthiness. I knew it to be a true and forever healing. Would those feelings creep in again? They would try to, but I knew the falsehoods they were and continued to shoo them away with God's truth.

Only when I surrendered could God work in me. I had been holding on to this for a lifetime, this familiarity of neediness, wanting, self-sacrificing. That night, I handed the pain, shame, anxiety, and heartache over to the only One who could heal me. And He did, He changed me.

Soon after this, the man I had been dating let me know he was seeing someone else. I was genuinely happy for him, because I knew he was not who God wanted to pair me with, and I was not the person he was looking for either. I wished him all the happiness God had in store. No hurt, no remorse, no feelings of abandonment or rejection, just happy. What a joyous feeling.

God took all the pain, failures, and mistakes to open my heart and mind, and allow me to fully surrender. I no longer needed acceptance from other people. It didn't matter if someone loved me or not, if someone or even no one valued me. It didn't matter whether I fit in with friends, with church, or with family. None of it mattered. God took the unhealthiness away.

I had to surrender to Him to change for what was to come. The life He would reveal in the months ahead was not like anything I had ever experienced. I would find it beyond anything I could imagine. Surrendering was just a step on the road to the new life He had in store.

Third Day's *Surrender* looped on my headphones. The group's CD *Move* was the first Christian music I purchased. The words sang of assurance and courage. It reinforced what I needed to work on—to give up my life, my thoughts, my old ways to the only One who could change me. It was time—time for me to surrender everything and allow God to forge me into His vision.

He continued to change and mold me as I continued to surrender. Then God laid out my road map.

Road Signs

In this story, God showed Michelle the strength of surrendering to Him. Her misconception of control equating to strength had to be corrected to move forward in her healing process.

Recall when nothing you did changed the outcome of a situation:

What events or life situations were happening during this time?

What actions did you take?

When looking back, is there anything you could have done differently to change the outcome?

What lesson can you take away from the outcome of the situation?

How do you think God used this situation in your life?

Yet you, Lord, are our Father.
We are the clay, you are the potter;
we are all the work of your hand.
Isaiah 64:8

Journal:

5
Road Map

Paul's Lesson:
Follow God's example, therefore, as dearly loved children and walk in the way of love, just as Christ loved us and gave himself up for us as a fragrant offering and sacrifice to God.
Ephesians 5:1-2

Traveling is fun, but it can be scary if you don't know where you are going. I was lost for so long I didn't know which way to turn, which direction to take. The best way to get back on track was a *road map*.

God offered methods of communication to know what I could expect on His Path. Foremost was the Bible. I read scripture daily. Once a week, I would have *sanctuary night* in which I read the Bible and wrote in my journal.

He gave me Christian friends who listened and advised. Most were from church and some were at work. They showed patience with me, but interjected when they believed I was misinterpreting God's direction for my life. Their reasoning came from scripture and was a valuable guide in my journey.

God drew me to read books, both on my own and as part of study groups. The books gave proper instruction on a variety of topics, including the Christian marriage. I read *The Power of the Praying Wife* by Stormie Omartian. What a testimony of praying for another expecting nothing in return. Powerful.

God led me to an abundance of Christian music. The music, I found, resonated in a way the spoken and written word could not. Music immersed me into a variety of messages God was delivering. Songs like *Beautiful* by MercyMe and *Garden* by Matt Maher showed how God saw me and how I should see myself. Music continues to enhance my faith life.

The most impactful events during this time was a class on marriage. It was held at the church I was attending. Since I had taken a class to learn to be a good dance partner, I was now wanting to learn to be a godly marriage partner. I had to learn how to be the wife He expected me to be. I had to forget all I had learned and experienced. None of it matched what I was about to gain.

A couple who had been married for over 20 years led the class. They were in love, and their interaction with each other gave me a comfort I could not explain. She respected him and he adored her. There were no games being played, there were no power struggles, no hidden agendas. How they were in front of the class was the same as when they were alone as a couple. This became clear soon after the class began.

We met in the basement of the church. He opened the first class by describing their life together, number of children, career paths, military duties, and general life structure surrounding their current relationship. She spoke about her changing roles as a spouse over the years while the husband sat attentive and listened. As she invited him to interject, he partnered with her in a beautiful picture of a happy couple.

I sat in a group of people from every background, all ages and seasons of life. I thought, *how can this Garden of Eden be true? How can two people stay content with each other for that long?* I didn't get it. There had to be problems, issues, tragedies, faults, arguments, something! But, at first, there was no sign of these events.

The second session was much of the same. Lessons on working things out, partnering with God to partner with each other, listening to class members talk of their issues and the teaching couple offering constructive advice on how to work things out.

Week after week, we sat together and listened to the *God* approach to marriage. It was a spiritual map of how to be a better partner and companion. I kept thinking *If their marriage has been this way all along, how easy to tell us how good it can be, how lovely and fulfilling.* I did not expect the story which unfolded near the end of the class sessions.

On the second to last week of class, the couple came in with a different demeanor. One of quiet resolve and purpose. It was not like them to be this way and was a little unnerving. What had happened? Were they fighting or arguing? The couple poised themselves and the husband began, "We have a powerful story to share with you and we want you to know only by God's Grace could we make it through."

I thought, *I knew it was too good to be true.*

The story they shared continues to affect me today. Early in their marriage before he became a Christian, the husband had an affair. Once he accepted Christ a few years after, he confessed to his wife and she forgave him.

Years later, he found out he had a child from the affair. Paternity tests confirmed parentage and he met his teenaged daughter for the first time. I watched his wife as he told the story of the initial betrayal and then the discovery of an unknown child. As the story continued, I expected some reaction from his wife—pain, sadness, anger. She listened and showed nothing but loving interest.

After he finished his version, his wife began with hers. She revealed the pain of unfaithfulness, the hard and long process of forgiveness, and the full acceptance of a grown child who was not biologically hers, but hers through love. She smiled throughout the talk, not one tear, frown, or hurtful look. This was a story of the essence of God's relationship with me.

I felt my face flush and turn red. My heart thumped a little faster. My eyes worked hard to hold back the tears. God's Love, His Grace, and Forgiveness was wrapped up in this couple's story. I saw the pureness of true forgiveness, the resolve of acceptance, and the love I had only read of—a love showing us how God loves us—unconditionally.

I left the class and walked across the cold, dark parking lot to my car. As I got in and started it up to warm the engine, I sat limp and spent. God had shown me how His Love completes a marriage, ordains it, sanctifies it in every way. The love and faith in God spills over into the love and faith in a partner. A commitment to God allows commitments to another effortless. Knowing His forgiveness for all we do allows us to forgive another.

Through the marriage class, the books I read, and other Christian couples I knew, God showed me marriage is sacred. It is also messy and hard and challenging. There are small annoyances and huge catastrophes along the way. The class was a road map for being God's first before partnering with someone else.

The wife and partner I had been in the past was far from the woman God was showing me now. He had given me the path to follow and the changes I needed to make to get to the destination He set before me. I was ready to learn more, be more, and become the version God intended.

I prayed daily for this future person, this unknown man. I didn't know who, when, where, or how, but I felt God had someone in mind. I prayed for and asked God to watch over him. How long would I wait? I didn't know and didn't care. I knew I had to become who God wanted me to be now and not wait one more minute. I committed even more to making the changes.

A few months later, God led me to the most dramatic change of all. He invited me to join Him in a covenant.

Road Signs

In the next step, Michelle discovered God had a plan to show her how to be a godly partner. Being a partner covers many roles, including spouse, family member, friend, or any close relationship.

Think of a partnership in your life, either current or past:

What role do you play in the relationship?

What do you expect to get out of the partnership?

What do you give to the other person?

What boundaries would you set up to create more balance?

How could you be more like God's version of you in the partnership?

A wife of noble character who can find?
She is worth far more than rubies.
Her husband has full confidence in her
and lacks nothing of value.
She brings him good, not harm,
all the days of her life.
She is clothed with strength and dignity;
she can laugh at the days to come.
Proverbs 31:10-12,25

Journal:

6
Covenant

Paul's Lesson:

Do you not know that your bodies are temples of the Holy Spirit, who is in you, whom you have received from God? You are not your own; 20 you were bought at a price. Therefore, honor God with your bodies.
1 Corinthians 6:19-20

My first introduction to sexuality was one of a biological role, an act of procreation of human beings and other animals. This was around the time my youngest sister, Sheila, would be born. My parents bought the elementary-aged books explaining the physiology of it all.

At five, I understood the concept of sex and the result was the birth an offspring. I confirmed my knowledge one afternoon by explaining to my mother our female dog was *getting her eggs fertilized* by a male dog in the backyard. "See?", I pointed out the window showing my mother the act which sparked my brilliant realization.

In the 1970s, the concept our bodies were gifts given for the honor and glory of God was not part of *normal* society. I grew up amid the sexual revolution, a time of sexual liberation and acceptance of sexual relationships outside of marriage. Nude adult photos and pornography became available through magazines and photos, some of which I saw as a child. The impact it had on me altered my self-view. The body was an object to be sought.

In my teenage years, after the molestation at fifteen, the concept of my body being valued, sacred and holy never entered my mind. I sought sexual attention from males and placed myself in degrading and abusive situations. I felt shame and remorse, yet compelled to repeat the pattern which resulted from the sexual trauma.

For the next 27 years, my relationships began as a physical relationship. Without sex, the relationships lacked the substance and depth of love and care I so longed to have. The basis for the relationship always went back to how it began, physically. Each pairing had a volatile foundation, under which circumstances would cause it to disintegrate and fall apart. All eventually did.

Physical intimacy was not a sacred celebration of a committed marriage by a God-bonded couple. I believed I could choose to do as I wanted with my body in a responsible manner. Match this with an unhealthy mind and broken self-image, and you get what I got—using physical intimacy to something other than what God intended.

Sex can be *used* in many ways—manipulation, enjoyment, expression of love, violence, power, stress-relief, procreation, fantasy, bribery, or as many ways as there are human beings on the earth.

God revealed during the first year of living with Him - sex does not equal love. Just because two people are physically intimate, does not mean emotional intimacy. Yet love can develop over time and have purpose and meaning, but the act of sex alone, in my experience, does not develop a relationship and is not the foundation God intended for me.

Part of my healing process was to look at how God viewed me, not as I had envisioned myself—an object of desire and lust, or to be used or abused. I was created to be cherished, revered, sacred and holy. But how could I become that vision of purity after decades of living far outside His image?

On May 16, 2011, during one of my journal sessions, God revealed His plan. I was to be His wife first—holy and irreproachable—in mind, spirit, and body. Committed to God alone, I had to become unconditionally His before I could share myself with another. And only with the man He chose for me.

In my journal, I wrote what God was sharing with me, "*Abstinence, celibacy is part of the sanctification of your relationship. It will be the testimony to share with others. Be mindful of your desires and understand it is part of being human, but you are Reborn in spirit and mind and body, this will keep you true to the commitment to Me.*" He continued, "*Our covenant will be sanctified so long as you honor, obey, and hold reverence for the sanctification. Strong hearts, solid foundation, spiritual intimacy, and deepest of love is what you will both receive and experience following My path.*"

One would think a message like that would adjust my thinking instantaneously. I laid out my struggle to God. I contemplated whether this covenant was even possible. My mind told me *No*, my body told me *Are you crazy*? To commit to this for an unknown amount of time was ludicrous. *How could I commit for that long? Was God tricking me to become a nun?* These thoughts flew around in my head.

God gave me clear direction—crystal clear. I was ALL IN, or His plan would not work. I had to commit and obey His course of action, or inaction in this case. Could I do this? Could I not have sex with anyone else or even with myself until I married again? Married? *Good Lord, help me please.* And who was this person? Who was He partnering me with? How would I know? My mind was in overdrive trying to reconcile this new notion.

For several days, I struggled, argued, countered, and negotiated. When something like sex has been a major part of life, to do without it is not only challenging, but also habit breaking, idol destroying, and a complete transformation of thought. It would take time to see His reason behind the covenant. He required my obedience in the moment, not my understanding.

I thought of this, prayed over it and gained the resolve I needed to commit and obey God's direction. In my journal entry a few days later, I fully accepted God's way and wholly gave myself to His plan, not only for the covenant but for all God wished to change in me.

I became all God's, no one else's, not even my own. I was passionately, completely His. I would obey His command and keep the covenant. The scripture He shared helped me to see how destructive I had been with my vision of sex and how I needed a complete reset in thinking to accept God's version of sexuality in my life. His perfect, spotless, precious, and holy version.

The scripture helped highlight the promise and how important it would be in the coming months and years. In Joshua 24:21-25, the nation of Israel made a vow—they chose God. Joshua confirmed the commitment and reiterated the people's promise, making sure he and God understood their pledge. The people, once more, vowed their allegiance to God, to obey Him, and to destroy all idols. This was their permanent and binding contract.

God said it would not be easy and, of course, He was right. I continued to focus my thoughts and gained a resolve my physiology would not define who I was or who God wanted me to be.

Living in His covenant became easier as each day passed. It was a mind-game to retrain my brain to think in God's way. I used scripture to help me through this time and replaced my unhealthy thinking. I exercised to relieve the stress and soon the desire left.

Eternal by Sanctus Real reminded me of the relationship I desired most of all. The love affair between me and God. He would never change and I wanted to be eternally His. I was on board for His plan and I knew I would keep the covenant.

Only when I was clearly on the other side of understanding my body was the temple of the Holy Spirit, could God introduce me to the man He had chosen for me. My *previous* self was not an acceptable version.

God had bigger plans than just healing my own unhealthy view of sexuality. He began by setting up the first meeting.

Road Signs

The step Michelle was led to during this time was the most challenging. God knew the right method to change her thinking and create a new person through the covenant. Michelle worked to realign her body image with God's view of her.

Contemplate a thought or perception of your body not aligned with how God sees you:

Name one negative thought about your body. Write it down.

If your closest friend said this about you, how would you feel?

What scripture can you find to counters the negative view of yourself?

What would God say to you if you declared this negative thought before His Throne?

Name five positive things about yourself and read these along with your chosen scripture for the next week, month or year - however long it takes to start seeing God's version of you.

It is God's will that you should be sanctified:
that you should avoid sexual immorality;
that each of you should learn to control your own body in a way that is holy and honorable,
not in passionate lust like the pagans, who do not know God;
1 Thessalonians 4:3-5

Journal:

7
First Meeting

Paul's Lesson:

Do not think of yourself more highly than you ought, but rather think of yourself with sober judgment, in accordance with the faith God has distributed to each of you.

Romans 12:3

The first time I met Greg was at a January 2011 employee activities committee meeting. A co-worker, Len, asked me to join the group as a representative for our floor. The committee planned and organized fun events such as ice cream socials, raffles, and picnics. Sub-committees then formed to execute each activity. Greg was acting chair and a leadership advocate for the group.

Each new member introduced themselves and I became *Michelle from the 7th floor.* There were others who had recently joined and each had a turn of introduction. Most of the committee members were women, with my 7th floor co-worker and Greg the only males.

I remember watching Greg during the first meeting and admiring how he listened to each opinion. He waited with patience for discussions to wane and a summarized a final consensus.

I took part in several more meetings and volunteered at the events each month. By March, however, my job role changed and I was bombarded with work. I excused myself from the planning meetings and events until I could regain control of my workflow.

I next attended a meeting in June 2011, and plans were well underway for the Fourth of July picnic. Each employee signed up, along with their family members, and would receive a wristband to enter the picnic grounds. Our sub-committee's job was to hand out the wristbands before the date and, on the day of, manage the cleanup during and after the event.

I volunteered to hand out the wrist bands along with Greg and another committee member, Crissy. We cannot tell the story of us without including the role Crissy played, though I didn't know the impact she had in our first conversation until much later.

I walked down a long inner stairway to the cafeteria where Greg and Crissy sat at a table. Boxes of envelopes were at the ready, each with tickets inside, and employee names and number of attendees were on a printed checklist for confirmation. I took a seat on one side, Greg on the other, and Crissy in the middle.

Crissy chatted with Greg as they had known each other for some time through the committee and other events.

Crissy said, "Greg, I have a lady friend you would like. She's the head of a charitable organization and is single. How would you like to meet her for dinner? A blind date?"

"Uh, hold on a minute," Greg stalled and then leaned into the conversation, "I am so busy with my new job, my kids just graduated high school, so much is happening in my life right now. I am flattered, but I am simply not interested. My life is pretty full and dating is just not on my list of things to add."

His expression was one of resolve, not apologetic in any form. Crissy laughed and said, "Ok, but if you ever change your mind, let me know. She's a great lady."

Greg reaffirmed his intent on bachelorhood and we continued to hand out wristbands. Crissy took her leave to go back to work and Greg and I managed the remaining distribution.

At church, I agreed to teach a class in the fall on health and well-being based on a book by Danna Demetre, *Change Your Habits, Change Your Life.* I read the book and it resonated with me to help reprogram my unhealthy thinking. I suggested it to the Adult Studies leadership for an eight-week course. They agreed and put it on the agenda.

The curriculum was geared more towards women, but anyone could attend the sessions and gain valuable instruction on how our brains work, how habits form, and what God can do to help us undo that which we do to ourselves—change bad habits to good.

I was ready for women to be a part of the class, but something nagged at me to gain resources in case men attended. I prayed about it on a Sunday night for God to send me a trusted, Christian man who would be a great resource for the male perspective. I knew God would connect me with someone, but I didn't know who or when.

The following Tuesday morning, with Crissy gone to her office, I turned to Greg and said, "I am teaching a class this fall for church and I am worried I would lack resources for any men who may attend."

Greg said, "You came to the right person." He told me of all the books he had, Christian books, books on self-help, and books to help men find God. I was floored. What I didn't know was, at the same moment Crissy left, God was having His own conversation with Greg. I found my trusted, Christian male friend, and Greg found much more.

In a thought not his own, in a still voice, this logical engineer heard God. *"If you see this woman as I see her, you will not help but to fall in love with her. Do you accept her as I show her to you now?"* His first thought was *YES.* His second thought was, *Boy, I'm going to end up in Human Resources so fast.*

As we talked, he did not indicate a Divine conversation had just transpired. He was still the same newly found friend I knew him to be. Nothing more. But one thing was different. I could not stop talking with him. The conversation flowed from life to the past, to self-discoveries, and then to God.

He asked where I lived and I shared with him I had moved a few months earlier from Petersburg to north of Richmond in an area called Short Pump. A look of curiosity crossed his face.

"Where exactly is your apartment?" he inquired. I told him the location, over by the Food Lion grocery store about a half mile from the library.

He smiled, "I live in an apartment about a half mile on the other side of the library."

Interesting, I thought, *we live about a mile apart.* Funny how I had never met him before January. "How long have you worked for the company?" I asked looking for more similarities.

"About five years here in the Richmond location."

"I've been here since the fall of 2006," I smiled, "Strange how we've never met each other until this year."

We packed up the remaining envelopes and cleared the table to head back to work. I followed him into the elevator and he stopped at the sixth floor, just below mine, and I followed him off the elevator—still talking, still listening, not wanting the conversation to end.

He offered me his email address in case I thought of questions about teaching the class from a male perspective. I came back to myself, a little embarrassed I followed him to his floor, and I said my goodbyes. He thanked me for talking with him and we parted ways.

I turned to the elevator as Greg headed through the door to his cubicle. I looked up as the elevator doors opened, "I don't know what You are doing, God, but I know You're up to something!"

This meeting, I realized later, was not only God's timing, but Greg's as well. He meant what he said about not looking for or wanting a relationship because his life was full and somewhat complicated.

If the meeting had happened earlier, I would not have been the person God wanted to introduce to Greg, the Michelle God wanted me to be. Greg also would not have been open to what God showed him that day—a future with me.

God had a plan for both of us and we didn't see it fully until He asked us the two questions.

Road Signs

In this step, God answered Michelle's prayers for a trusted male Christian friend, but His plans were so much more. It wasn't until later Michelle discovered God's plan was far beyond anything she could imagine.

Think a moment or situation in which you know God answered your prayers:

What was the situation? Write it down.

What prayer did you say during this time?

How did God respond to your prayer? Or not respond?

Looking back, how has the answered, or unanswered, prayer affected you or your life?

What changes in you or your life did you see from this experience?

What we have received is not the spirit of the world, but the Spirit who is from God, so that we may understand what God has freely given us.
1 Corinthians 2:12

Journal:

____

____

____

____

____

____

8
Two Questions

Paul's Lesson:
The person without the Spirit does not accept the things that come from the Spirit of God but considers them foolishness, and cannot understand them because they are discerned only through the Spirit. The person with the Spirit makes judgments about all things, but such a person is not subject to merely human judgments,
1 Corinthians 2:14-15

God's reassurance with each step of healing showed me a Love never ending and perfect in every way. This was the point of the journey in which God inserted Greg into my life. From the first conversation at the wristband table, to volunteering at the company picnic, and exchanges of several emails, all led to the first walk together. A few weeks had passed and we met one evening at the library.

This was the first of many moments of walking and talking, sharing ourselves and partaking in a deep, spiritual dialog. I had experienced nothing like this—this spiritual intimacy. Each step and word was meaningful, purposeful, and important.

During the first walk, I shared every past moment I could think of hoping to show him my true self. For him to understand who I was now, he had to know who I had been before finding God. I wanted Greg to know the bad parts about my past, the good parts, and my experiences with God, up to that point.

Next came our first full day together - I guess we could call it our first official date. It began early one Saturday morning at the Subway halfway between our apartments. He bought breakfast for us and we sat at a booth by the window. As he reached across the table to hold my hand, he bowed his head to pray. He said a blessing over our food and thanked God for our time together. We ate and then walked for several hours.

After the walk, we stopped by his apartment to get a drink of water and cool off. It was mid-July and warm. He showed me the floor to ceiling bookshelves full of resource books he spoke of at our first meeting. I met his little poodle, Sandy, and his cat, Marvin. We sat and talked more. He invited me to go swimming and we spent the afternoon lounging by the pool.

"Would you like to go out to dinner and see a movie tonight?" he asked, smiling.

"Sure, I'd love to, but I need to go back to my apartment to change. I can walk back now and be ready before you pick me up," I answered.

"Let me go check on my poodle and change, too. Then I'll drive you over to your apartment and you can get ready while I wait," he countered.

Anyone else would think this was a classic move to get a woman alone in her apartment. This was not Greg's motive. His gentlemanly manners were impeccable. He was just thinking through the evening and figured out the most efficient way to manage time.

We walked from the pool to his apartment with towels in tow. I felt safe with Greg, this I knew. I sat on the couch to wait while he showered and changed. Both pets stopped by to greet me like old friends. Sandy laid beside me in comfort and Marvin strolled through to let me know he was present. Sweet pets, easy to love them.

Greg announced he was ready to take me over to my place so I could get ready. Roles reversed, he sat on my couch while I showered and changed. The ease I felt around him was unmistakable. He was a protector, a watchman, trusted and certain. He was my friend.

We went to a great Mexican restaurant, my favorite food besides bacon. We sat across from each other as we had that morning over breakfast. When the food arrived at the table, he reached his hand to mine. We bowed our heads to pray blessings for the food and thankfulness for the day spent.

After the movie, he drove to my apartment. We realized we had been together for the last fourteen hours. Eating, walking, talking, laughing, getting to know one another and sharing our thoughts, fears, history, and life.

As he walked me to my door he said, "We probably have talked more in the last day than most married couples do in years."

"Yes, I guess you're right. I have talked with you more today about things I never talked about to anyone," I answered.

"Thank you for today," he smiled.

"Thank you, also, for a wonderful day." I smiled back.

You would imagine this would be a perfect moment for a good night kiss, and it may have been, but it didn't happen. It wasn't supposed to happen. Not at this moment. A kiss would have told me all I saw in this man's motives was a means to an end, that his intentions were not as honorable as I suspected, and that he was just putting on a front to get close. You know, like other men.

No, there was no kiss, no touch, no hand holding, except for the prayers. The happenings of this day would carry through to the next time we were together, walking, talking, and sharing life. We shared with words, with thoughts, with spiritual intimacy, not with physical touch. It was purposeful and part of who I had become.

I belonged to God, now, and was not my own to give permission for contact, for kissing, for even hand holding. Greg never attempted, never tried to overstep any boundaries. I had not discussed with him my covenant with God. It was a silent understanding my body was a sacrament.

After about six weeks, we became great friends. He attended my church. We went to Sunday School and services together. He joined in on the church projects, including starting a cafe before Contemporary Service. He brewed the coffee and I managed the operations.

We met for lunch at work, not hiding our new-found relationship from anyone. We carpooled in since we lived so close to each other. Each day after work, we would meet up for a long walk, unless we had other obligations, family events, or appointments.

The evening walks were the best. Sandy would tag along for the first mile, then we would swing by his apartment and drop her off. We would pound out another few miles, following endless sidewalks through the neighborhoods. The route would always run us by my apartment so he would see me there safely before heading home.

One Sunday afternoon, he was spending the day with his son at the driving range. I was at my apartment doing laundry after church. In my tiny laundry room, I stood in front of the washing machine loading it full of dirty, sweaty clothes and God asked me a question.

It was the same feeling I had in the wee hours of the morning when He asked me to go get my grandfather's Bible.

I had a warm feeling well up inside and the thought was not my own. It resonated, like before, from outside in, like the words enveloped my head and heart at the same time. A tapping at my spirit.

"Would you take this relationship, just as things are now, with no physical contact, for the rest of your life if that's what I wanted for you?"

I did not hesitate. The answer was *YES*. "Yes, Lord, yes, I will," I said out loud. I buckled to my knees, tears flowed like rain. Overwhelmed, I realized how much God had changed me, how complete was His healing, and how different were my desires.

With everything I was, I wanted this—this dearest friend God had brought to my life. I was willing to have nothing more than what already existed between us. It was perfect, beautiful, and holy. Yes, I wanted this. I sat down on the linoleum and laughed. I laughed at how perfect God is.

Then, I had to tell Greg of the covenant, of the promise I made. I knew it may change things between us, but I had to let him know. After all we had discussed and shared, I had not shared the covenant with him and it was time.

The Monday after the laundry room experience, Greg and I didn't carpool as usual. I drove separate that day and cannot remember why. We did not see each other at work and then, as I headed home, I got a text: *Would you like to walk with me this evening*?

I responded: *Yes. I think it will rain, but I want to walk anyway.*

I do, too. I will meet you halfway.

Ok, see you in a few, I sent back.

I changed quickly, popped my headphones in, and cranked up my walking music - a Christian band blared into my brain. I walked fast and weaved my way through the middle neighborhood to land in front of the library. Greg was there ready to slow his pace for my short stride. He is 6'3" and my 5'4" stature cannot keep up without a jog.

I put my headphones away and we talked about our day, work, kids, pets, life once more. The words were free and comfortable between us. For the first time, I was a little nervous. I needed to tell him about the covenant, but how was he going to react? Would he think me foolish? Would he accept it and reassure me we would stay friends? Would he think it was the dumbest thing he'd ever heard and run the other way? *Most men would, you know, run far, far away and never look back,* I thought to myself.

We headed over to a shaded street just in case the rain came, and it did—heavy and fast. We ran under the largest tree we could find and stood close to the trunk. Drips came through, but the branches were full enough to be a makeshift umbrella.

I looked up at him and said, "There's something I have to tell you."

"Ok," he hesitated as this is the precursor statement to every bad piece of news ever.

"It's not bad," I assured him, "At least, I don't think so."

"Alright, I am listening," he said and stood with his hands on his hips waiting for the bomb I was about to drop.

"I made a covenant with God. I cannot have sex, either with someone else or with myself, until I am married," I said as clear and concise as I could muster.

"Oh, wow," he muttered, "Ok. Hmm."

And that was it. He said nothing more. The rain let up, the sun came out, and we continued our walk, the same as every time before. He walked me to my apartment and we said good night. Then he walked home.

I didn't know what to expect afterwards. I had no inclination if he would accept it, reject it, or if it really mattered at all. He might not talk to me ever again or he might continue to be the same, dear friend he had been from the beginning. I had no clue, so I waited.

Two days later, I had an evening to myself. Wednesdays were sanctuary nights. I would journal and read the Bible. I dedicated the three to four hours to spending time with God. I wrote of my innermost feelings, struggles, and worries, and listened for God to guide me through scriptures and prayer.

This evening, I was about two hours into the sanctuary time when I receive a text. Greg was out walking alone and asked if he could stop by my apartment for a few minutes. I sent a text back saying it was fine and put my notebook and Bible away before his arrival.

I heard a knock on the door and I opened it to find Greg dripping with sweat. He accepted a glass of water I offered and sat on the couch. I turned sideways to look at him, my knees were bent with my feet pushed into the cushion.

"How are you?" I started the conversation.

"I am fine. I just needed to come talk with you." he said.

"Oh, and what do you need to talk about?" I inquired, thinking he came to tell me he no longer wanted to spend time together or be friends with such a strange person. I prepared myself for what may come next.

"I was out walking and," he continued, "I had a conversation with God. As I walked God said, '*Are you willing to accept this covenant with her?*'"

I sat in stunned silence. He went through his thought processes in those few days: why I would agree to such a thing as celibacy, was I having serious issues, or was this just part of my relationship with God? All the while, I was imagining his answer to the question: yes, no, or she's nuts and I want no part of this.

I knew Greg may run the other way and never look back, but there was a glint of hope he would understand my position, my commitment and all I had been through.

Greg continued, "I have thought long and deep about this and, when I knew God wanted me to answer, I realized I don't have to understand why you made this commitment, I have to decide if I accept it or not." He paused, staring at me. I saw no sign from his expression whether his answer was yes or no.

"Well?" I threw out there, "What is your answer?" I sat hugging my knees close to my chest.

"Before I answer, I believe God is leading you to a choice, a pretty powerful one. I feel you will choose between two things, and I am not sure what that is, but it is still a choice." This would have seemed cryptic, but I believed he had picked up on the laundry room experience - something I had not shared yet. He did not know I had already made the choice. I accepted what God had given us, this beautiful, deeply spiritual, and intellectual relationship.

Finally, he said, "Again, I have thought through this and I accept this covenant between you and God. I will honor and respect it."

What happened next was one of the most remarkable experiences of my life. As he was saying the words, the acceptance, the affirmation—I watched a thin veil lift between us. I cannot find the words to describe it any other way. In that moment, God fully revealed who Greg was and I fell in love with him.

From the January introduction to the God meeting the following June, until that moment in mid-August, God had filtered us—or at least me—only lifting the unknown veil when the two questions were answered. Would I accept this relationship just as it was, and would he accept my covenant with God? It was as if, through our collective choices, a protective shield dissolved.

God showed me through my question how much I had truly changed. Matt Maher's *Alive Again* reminded me what changed and how God opened my ears and eyes to see His plan. In Greg's question, God verified this man was of His choosing. Only then, with trust secured for my Creator and my dearest friend, was I ready for biggest question of all.

Road Signs

This step showed Michelle how profound her perception had changed. By following God's plan, she discovered her wants aligned with what God set before her. She realized a healthier version of herself did exist.

Remember a time when you aligned yourself with God, in action or thought.

Write about the alignment.

What changed in your thinking to be able to align with God?

What challenges did you face in aligning your thought or action with God's direction?

How did it feel to follow God's plan?

What results came from aligning with God?

Trust in the Lord with all your heart and lean not on your own understanding; in all your ways submit to him, and he will make your paths straight.
Proverbs 3:5-6

Journal:

9
Do You Believe?

Paul's Lesson:

To the praise of his glorious grace, which he has freely given us in the One he loves. In him we have redemption through his blood, the forgiveness of sins, in accordance with the riches of God's grace that he lavished on us. With all wisdom and understanding
Ephesians 1:6-8

Now that I had given myself to God fully and completely, it was time to ask the question. What God did for me was miraculous and extensive. He guided my heart to trust Him in all things. His immeasurable Love nurtured my walled up, tucked away heart that trembled with every new awakening.

First, had come to know God. Once I believed God was real and He loved me immensely, unconditionally, and completely, only then could I believe in His Son Jesus Christ. For if I believed God Loved me, how could I not believe He would send His Only Son to die for me to give me everlasting life with Him for eternity?

To not believe in Jesus would mean I did not believe in the perfect Love of my Father in Heaven. It meant I didn't believe in redemption, forgiveness, salvation, mercy, grace, or anything else that God gave us through Christ. To believe in Jesus meant I fully accepted God for who He says He is, for what He has done for me, and for His Perfect Love.

For years, I could not believe this happened to others. Stories I heard of people believing and changing through accepting Christ I categorized as fairy tales. When others would tell me someone I had known became a Christian and changed, I was a skeptic.

"I can't believe it," I would say, "Do you know who she was? Do you know what she did? That's hard for me to accept. Becoming a Christian wouldn't change someone that much."

I dispelled the belief that Jesus could change someone from a broken, terrible, imperfect person into one who is forgiven, full of grace, and reborn, until it happened to me. I had to decide. Did I believe Jesus died for me? Did Jesus exist? Is Jesus who He said He is or was He a made-up story that somehow survived for 2,000 years?

When I began my relationship with Greg, he noticed one thing about me when I spoke of my relationship with God. All along in this book, you have read much about God, but little about Jesus, until this chapter. There was a reason for that. Although I had a new relationship of God, and I believed Jesus was the Son of God, I did not have a personal understanding of Jesus.

Can this be true that one can have such a transformative and profound relationship with God, yet not have a close and personal understanding of Jesus? My answer is *yes* and *no.*

Yes, one can know of someone without understanding the depths and intricate aspects of who they are—an acquaintance. A somewhat familiar figure, yet not connected on a deeper level. And *no,* until I knew Jesus Christ as my Savior, I could not begin to know the lengths and depths of how God felt about me.

A couple of months after our first date, Greg drove his son to pick up a rental car. It was late in the evening and he asked me to ride along so he could introduce us. After Greg dropped off his son, we headed back to my apartment. As Greg turned onto the main street, God shared with me, *Talk to Greg about marriage.*

I wrestled with God.

Really? Lord, why do you do this to me? I cannot and will not talk to him about marriage; we just started dating. The timing is all wrong. Why would you ask me to talk with him about that? We haven't even kissed each other, for goodness sake.

Greg sensed something and asked me if I was alright.

I said, "I am wrestling now. God is asking me to talk with you about something and I don't want to."

He knew what that meant with our hours and hours of conversations. It was not the first time God had jumped in to orchestrate a conversation between us. Greg gave me time and peace to work through what God was sharing with me. I sat quietly with my hands clasped tight.

Even as I felt my struggling subside, I continued my argument, *I cannot talk to him about marriage. This is nuts! Why are you asking me to do this? It is way too soon and this doesn't seem right.*

Again, the God clearly conveyed, "*Talk to him about marriage.*" Finally, my wrestling ceased and I complied.

"God wants me to talk to you about marriage," I revealed, my hands still holding each other.

Greg replied, "Funny you should bring it up. I have been meaning to talk to you about this for a week, now."

"Really!" I said shocked. Any leftover tension faded, and my hands unclenched.

Greg explained, "I wasn't sure how to bring this up and I don't want you to think this was too fast, but I felt compelled to talk to you about marriage."

I did not understand where this was going. Was he going to propose right now? Impossible! That couldn't be it. I wasn't ready for that.

"When you get married again, you need to wear a white dress," he offered.

"A white dress?" I questioned. "There is no way I would wear white! I have a child and was married twice before. Too much has happened in my life. It wouldn't be right," I answered. Defending my answer, I thought of the molestation, the situations I placed myself in over the years—how could I consider this? My thoughts countered his recommendation.

Greg continued, "You should wear white and here is why. If you truly believe Jesus Christ died for you, has washed you clean by His blood, has forgiven you of all your sins, and you are reborn through Him, then you will wear white on your wedding day."

Stunned, I collapsed internally and wept. This was not about a marriage to each other, this was about the bride and the Bridegroom. Love crashing through to my spirit, my body, my mind—I felt my heart explode!

I knew—knew–Jesus Christ died for me. Me. This broken, tattooed, twice divorced, queen of sinners. He loved me and it was personal. I was not just one of the millions over the millennia. Jesus loved me, died for me, rose again for me, forgave me, sanctified me, saved me, washed me clean, and made me new.

It was a moment of choice, a monumental decision—did I believe who Jesus was or did I not? God led me to the Bridegroom, to Jesus. I believed He was all He said He was and I would wear white on my wedding day, whenever it may be.

In the months after this poignant moment, God began the knitting.

Road Signs

The most important step God set before Michelle was to decide how she saw Jesus and what Christ meant to her personally. Coming to the revelation, Michelle's relationship with God through Christ became deeper and more meaningful.

Think of Jesus on a personal level, as if He were sitting beside you in this moment:

Who is Jesus to you?

When you talk or pray to God, how does Jesus show up your prayers?

What role does Jesus play in your relationship with God?

How differently do you see Jesus when you think of His sacrifice in first person as in Paul's words below?

What steps can you take to cultivate a personal relationship with Jesus Christ?

I have been crucified with Christ and I no longer live, but Christ lives in me. The life I now live in the body, I live by faith in the Son of God, who loved me and gave himself for me.
Galatians 2:20

Journal:

____

10
The Knitting

Paul's Lesson:

The Spirit searches all things, even the deep things of God. For who knows a person's thoughts except their own spirit within them? In the same way no one knows the thoughts of God except the Spirit of God.
1 Corinthians 2:10-11

How well do we know someone? Better yet, how well do we know ourselves? The more God worked in me, the greater I understood who I was and how I thought. Most of my self/God discoveries led to work, hard intentional work. I challenged myself to rewrite the image of who I had been and allowed God to show me other facets of Michelle—His Michelle.

God used this method as Greg and I got to know each other. One of the first exercises Greg and I did was to take the *5 Love Languages®* official assessment online[4]. We both read the book *The 5 Love Languages* by Gary Chapman before so we had a good background on the method. We all change over time and circumstance, so we took the test separately, then discuss the findings.

If you haven't read the book or taken the test, the premise is that we each have our own love language and if we are not getting the proper love speak in our lives; we don't feel loved—even if our partner is showing love in their own way. Our partner may show love differently than how we perceive it. It doesn't look like love even when they love us.

I read the book the summer after my second divorce and found I was not providing the love my ex-spouse needed and he was not providing what I needed to feel loved. Both of us were showing love in a way in which neither of us felt loved—but we had not realized it. Knowing this afterwards was revealing, but it would not fix the many problems my second marriage faced. I often wonder if I had known before the second marriage all the things God showed me later, would I have made the same choices?

I sat down at the computer in my apartment and took the assessment. I focused on answering each one honestly. The results were the same as the year before when I read the book and took the test on paper—physical touch. The other aspects of love languages mattered somewhat and were in this order - words of affirmation—words matter, quality time is nice, acts of service are valuable, but one thing didn't matter at all—receiving gifts. This was the least of all five and didn't even register in the results.

I had my list of love language priorities ready to compare with Greg's hoping at least some of the categories aligned. A few days later, Greg and I met for lunch downtown to analyze the findings. I went first and divulged my top element of love language—physical touch. He stopped me there and said, "Mine is physical touch, too."

"Oh, wow. How about the other categories? What percentage did the other one show?" I asked to see how close our results compared.

"Well, quality time is a second, then words of affirmation, acts of service, and last was receiving gifts," he revealed.

"That is close to mine," I exclaimed as I rattle off my list in order of importance. The quality time and words of affirmation were reversed in importance, but the last two categories were the same.

I laughed, "It's physical touch. God, the Great Comedian. We are in a covenant, no sex until marriage, and we both value and feel loved the most by physical touch."

It would be a disturbing joke if we had not understood God's plan in our relationship. We smiled at each other and finished our lunch before walking back to work. We held hands the whole way as we usually did. Our physical touch, the simple language of our love, now meant more than before lunch. It was saying *I love you* with a simple intertwining of fingers.

Other aspects of our likes and dislikes came forward as we had evenings and weekends to spend time together. Our conversations centered on relationship building, but would venture off to more mundane topics like Star Trek original or Next Generation, best Star Wars movie, favorite meal to eat, favorite to cook, and so on.

To help this *getting to know one another* along, Greg sent me a series of emails with open ended questions. He provided his answers and I would respond with my own. Some of the questions were conversation starters while others were basic information. Although I no longer have those questions and didn't save them, I know it allowed us to get to know one another and gave us insight.

Getting to know someone can intimidate us, especially when we feel like we could be judged for our preferences and idiosyncrasies. The exercises helped us became familiar with one another and encouraged us to be open with our inner selves. The answers came without fear of rejection and were fun.

God's lesson in this segment of our relationship? Knitting. God was joining us together through conversations and sharing. The knitting was a purposeful coming together of two people in a short amount of time to build a strong foundation.

We needed to be assured of acceptance, familiarity, and trust with our innermost nuances. We showed each other who we were when no one was looking. We exposed parts of ourselves that only God knew and we accepted those aspects of each other.

God led us to see each other for who we were without judgement. We knew more about one another in those few months than we knew about most people we had known for years. The knitting brought us closer and gave us an appreciation of how God sees us—as His precious children—loved no matter what. He knows us intimately and completely.

God showed us how to connect with each other on a deeper level. Without the physical intimacy that most couples share, our need for intimacy changed to emotional, intellectual, and spiritual. God provided the foundation that would carry us through the dramatic changes yet to come.

The knitting structured our relationship to enter the engagement.

Road Signs

Michelle discovered God wanted her to see a version of herself and of Greg she would not have seen otherwise. The purposeful questions and conversations allowed both Greg and Michelle to discover a deeply spiritual and intellectual understanding of one another.

Think of the closest relationship you have with another person:

Who is the person? Write the name or relationship.

Name one thing do they NOT know about you?

What would they think of you if they found out?

What positive outcome would occur once they knew?

How could God use this unknown thing to draw you closer or have a better understanding of each other?

You know when I sit and when I rise;
you perceive my thoughts from afar.
You discern my going out and my lying down;
you are familiar with all my ways.
Before a word is on my tongue
you, Lord, know it completely.
Psalm 139:2-4

Journal: ______________________________

____

____

____

____

11
The Engagement

Paul's Lesson:
My goal is that they may be encouraged in heart and united in love, so that they may have the full riches of complete understanding, in order that they may know the mystery of God, namely, Christ, in whom are hidden all the treasures of wisdom and knowledge.
Colossians 2:2-3

The months following were purposeful, intentional, and necessary. We said *I love you* for the first time. Public displays of affection were rampant with constant hand holding. We continued to have hours, weeks, months of conversations.

I thought the covenant would be easy. *Maybe I won't be attracted to him* or *God will give me great resolve NOT to think about sex,* I thought. Several weeks after expressing our love for one another, we kissed. I knew attraction was there. I also knew keeping this covenant would not be easy, but it would be crucial in God's plan for our relationship.

We spent days together, riding to work, walking in the evening, and taking moments to enjoy being with each other. Physically, we kissed and held hands. Mentally, we had a wide range of discussions from Star Trek episodes to US History to stories from the Bible. Spiritually, we focused on what God had planned for us. We knew God was working on a future life, but we didn't understand the details.

Greg and I spoke about marriage once or twice after that night of the white wedding dress episode. I mentioned to Greg that, when he felt the time was right to ask, I would like a necklace instead of a ring. I explained, "After my grandmother died, I had her gold cross necklace, but lost it, somehow. I loved that necklace. Even though I wasn't a Christian back then, I wore it. The cross was simply made, gold with a diamond in the middle, and it was beautiful. It was a sentimental piece and I am sad it's gone. I have only a few items to remember her by," I finished. Greg pondered in silence, as he usually did, but I trusted he heard me.

Months before, I realized Greg listened to most everything I said. Everyone who knows me long enough understands how much I love bacon. Any is fine, thick sliced, thin and crispy, smoked, hickory, but my favorite is pepper cured. Oh, my mouth waters as I write.

I believe I have long-forgotten DNA strand from my grandfather who grew up in West Virginia. His favorite time of year was late fall—hog killing time or hog butchering days. The communal ritual of the preparation for winter months. Smoked or salted, the ham hocks, bacon, chops, and shoulders were preserved to sustain the families. I can see how this may have attributed to my affinity for pork.

Flowers, chocolates, candies—these may be the first items a man presents a woman during the time of courtship. Greg called me one Saturday afternoon and said, "I have a present for you."

"A present? Okay," I responded, not knowing what to expect.

"I've been working on it all afternoon," he teased.

"Really! Hmm, I guess I will find out when you get here," I said expectantly. He planned to take me to dinner and then to a movie and would arrive within an hour to pick me up. I finish getting ready and thought of a list of things he might present as a token of caring.

I do love chocolate and flowers are nice, I thought to myself, but neither resonated. I resolved I would smile upon receiving such gifts. I would thank him and we would continue our evening together. As I gathered my purse, Greg knocked announcing his arrival. I opened the door and found him standing in front of me with a large, sealed container and a wide grin.

He handed me the gift and said, "I hope you like it." I must have looked confused because he smiled even more.

"What is this?" I asked.

"Open it," he said, "I took two hours to make it." The aroma caught my nose.

I ripped open the lid to reveal two pounds of pepper cured bacon, crispy and dark brown.

"You brought me BACON!" I exclaimed.

He laughed, "I did. I listened." And he was right, he heard me, he listened to what I said. I could not recall any one moment in which I explained my love for bacon, much less peppered bacon, but I am sure I talked about it. He heard me and responded. *Wow,* I thought, *he really is the best.*

In November, Greg invited me over to watch Monday Night Football. I arrived to have the pets greet me thoroughly. Greg served baked chicken, which tasted just like fried with his special recipe, some pasta and vegetables. The poodle, Sandy, danced around the table, as was her typical routine, to see if the added movement would either prompt something to fall on the floor or a giving hand would offer the tasty treat the nose told her was there.

After dinner, we settled on the love seat as the team kicked off the first quarter on the television. I like football, live or televised. I don't have a favorite team, I have a favorite player position, the kicker. It is all or nothing. Either they kick the ball and make an extra point or three, or nothing. It's finite; the ball goes through the uprights or it doesn't. The kicker can be a hero or a scoundrel, hoisted on shoulders or shunned in locker room. I have empathy for the kicker. No matter which team plays, I want the kicker to score.

To know Greg is to know he loves sports, especially hockey, but football is a close second. He listens to, watches, and reads sports news. I learned when he was watching a sporting event for full and clear communication to be heard, a commercial must be on—there must be a pause in the action or whatever I say falls into an abyss.

This night was no different, I assumed. I sat on the red leather loveseat, engrossed in the game with several kicker moments holding my attention. Greg sat next to me holding my hand and talking up the game action. Then suddenly, he turned and looked at me.

"Michelle," he said, "Will you consider becoming my wife?" Just like that, mid-game—full attention. I looked at him as he reached into his pocket and pulled out a box, a jewelry box, and opened it. Rather than a ring, it was an engagement necklace—a slender, silver, wispy cross. It was delicate and lovely.

My expression must have been a mixture of surprise and happiness. I took the cross pendent and said, "Yes, I would love to be your wife." And that was that. We kissed and laughed. Having this question asked during Monday Night Football was the best, and not even during a commercial. It was a self-focused moment amid one thing which holds his attention the most.

We went straight into discussion of living arrangements. It would be a financial advantage and convenient to either live in his one-bedroom apartment or find a two bedroom in the same complex. We both agreed, but God had His own plans.

Home became a different meaning than what either of us expected it to be. In December, Greg would move from his apartment to the house in which his grown children lived and he had shared with his first wife. Within a few days of the decision, they traded living spaces, she moved into the apartment as he moved into the house. They agreed this arrangement would be best for her and for their children, who were not ready to live on their own.

When Greg approached me with the subject, I knew God was unfolding His plan. Greg informed me of the decision they both made for themselves and their children. It made sense. Would it be challenging? Yes, but I knew God was working on this arrangement for all of us.

My son, David, had moved in with me a few months before to get back on his feet after a divorce. Three of Greg's adult children and his grandson lived in the house. After we married, all of us would live under one roof. It was an instant blended family with various ranges of personalities and issues. It would be stressful and chaotic, but we knew God would be there to guide us.

In late December, we took a trip to see his parents. The 12-hour drive from Virginia to Florida gave us many hours to talk. Somewhere in North Carolina as we traveled down I-95, Greg suggested we set the wedding date. We contemplated several weekends in the spring. He suggested a Saturday in March and I looked up the dates on my cell phone to see what dates showed. We discovered one of the Saturdays was March 17th, St. Patrick's Day.

We pondered how scheduling a wedding on St. Patrick's Day would work for others. Some guests would go out that night, so a morning wedding would be appropriate. But not too early, as people with children would have a hard time and so would we. A time closer to lunch sounded great.

We would serve a nice meal if we could work out a catering arrangement. The church had Wednesday night dinners with a fabulous team cooking tasty dishes each week, named The Bistro. I would call Missy, who led the kitchen staff during the dinners, to see if we could hire the team to prep and serve lunch for our guests.

We talked and turned each item over to see how the pieces fit. By the time we reached his parent's place, we had most every detail decided. The wedding would be at 11:00 a.m., no presents—we would request donations to be given to one of our four favorite charities, and we would ask the church to help us with catering, serving and planning.

Greg had told me stories of his mother, Sarah, and step-father, Ron, and their life together. They were married for nearly 30 years when Sarah was diagnosed with Alzheimer's. Ron, a pharmacist, managed her care by hiring five part-time care givers who took several hours shifts each weekday to cook, clean, and care for her.

Ron partnered with Sarah's doctors to find the right and most effective series of prescriptions to keep this terrible disease from stealing her life and mind. She declined over the years, but not as fast as most with the illness. Sarah still was conversational even if she didn't remember the sentence she said five minutes prior.

We pulled up to his parent's house. We stepped into the beautiful Spanish style home and it was immaculate. Not just one room, but every room was decorated for the holidays. There were five Christmas trees, each decorated by Ron and every ornament lovingly placed for Sarah's enjoyment.

As Ron brought us through the elegant dining room and down the hall to my room for the weekend, he gave Greg an update on Sarah's recent condition.

"She's been doing well lately. The first lady comes in around 5:00 a.m. to start breakfast and to do light cleaning. She helps her out of bed, bathes her and gets her dressed." He continued to describe his wife's daily routine, who comes when and what chores they do. Most of the team were home-school moms who enjoyed earning a little money and working a few hours a day.

"Her memory is fading, though," he explained, trying to soften the potential disappointment if she didn't recognize her oldest son. Greg understood. I left my suitcase in the bedroom and Greg continued to carry his through the kitchen to the family room where he would bed down for the night.

Meeting Ron and Sarah for the first time was a treasure and a challenge. Sometimes, when I am around new people, I withdraw and become a spectator. I engaged in polite conversation, but wanted to get to know these two through observation.

Greg walked with me around the family room, then the kitchen and beyond, to show off his mother's paintings. Greg had two of his mother's pieces at home and I recognized the pastel abstracts. How talented she was with both abstracts and landscape scenes. Her creations hung throughout the house and was reminiscent of an art gallery.

Returning to the family room, I said to Ron, "What beautiful work she created."

"She enjoyed it so much," he responded and pointed out the last few she completed before the disease halted her creativity.

"Did she ever think about selling her paintings?" I asked.

"Oh no, she painted because she loved it," he answered smiling. He enjoyed Sarah being who she was.

We soon took the visit from the family room to the covered pool area. Sarah settled in a chair facing the pool and the yard beyond. Greg, Ron, and I talked about work life, memories of Greg's children, updates on the kids and on. Sarah sat quietly looking at tropical plants and the pool water rippling in the breeze. Ron would reach over often and stroke her arm. She would look over at him and smile. "You ok, honey?" he would check. Sometimes she would nod, sometimes not.

I watched this interaction between Ron and Sarah, a loving touch, a kind word, a reassurance he was close, it was constant and comforting. Just as a parent understands the nuances of their toddler who can't quite communicate needs, Ron intuitively watched Sarah to find an expression or verbalization showing what she may need—too hot, too cold, hungry, tired. Caregiver—a small word for the enormity of who he truly was to her.

The afternoon tropical breeze was counterintuitive for December in Virginia, but not in Florida. We sipped iced tea and continued our conversation, pausing long enough for the check-ins with Sarah. Suddenly, she looked over at Ron and said, "My son is coming to see me."

Ron asked, "Which one honey?"

"Greg. My son, Greg, is coming to see me," she responded.

Ron smiled, "Well, honey, look right over there." He pointed in our direction to focus her gaze. She turned her head and said, "Oh, you are here!" She laughed and we all joined in for a moment. It was humor amid a heartbreaking disease. Our visit resumed and Sarah went back into her world once more.

Towards the end of our visit, I realized I had met one of the kindest and spiritually minded spouses. Ron lived the truest love - for better, for worse, in sickness, and in health, 'til death do us part. This was his covenant with God and his wife. It was his privilege to care for her - a true privilege. It was my privilege to witness.

Throughout our engagement, God showed up with affirmations of a relationship that was His design. A listening, giving, and caring partnership; an honoring of the loving connection that developed between us. We met each relational challenge with openness and a commitment to understanding. We listened to the other's point of view and came to a consensus.

God gave us an example of a Christian couple in Greg's parents, a true devotion to each other despite what life brings. Each challenge met with Grace that comes from living in Christ. A promise to honor and cherish, a covenant lived out daily, and a stewardship of the life God created.

On the drive home to Virginia, Greg and I conversed about the weekend, the loving relationship Ron and Sarah shared, the faith that Ron carried in his mission as her caregiver, and how Greg cherished who his step-father was to him and his mother.

Jesus said the two greatest commandments are to love God with all we are and to love each other as we love ourselves. Greg's stepfather Ron lived it—this love of God and of others. He vowed to live each moment with love at the forefront—regardless of whether the engagements were filled with disease, confusion, and disability. It was beautiful to witness. This is a lesson Greg and I both commit to in our marriage.

We talked more of the upcoming wedding and how we believed God wanted to orchestrate the day. We did not understand how lovely our wedding day would be, but first, there was the matter of the wedding dress.

Road Signs

Michelle learned in this step God's plan to ensure a stable and foundationally sound marriage. God showed Michelle how to be engaged in the relationship and offered wonderful examples of others showing the same.

Think of a relationship you have, personal, family, church or community.

What type of relationship is it?

What role do you play in the relationship?

How does God use you in this relationship?

What adjustments in thinking may be necessary to bring the relationship to more aligned with God's intent?

Name five things you can do to support the relationship in a healthy manner.

"Teacher, which is the greatest commandment in the Law?"
Jesus replied: "'Love the Lord your God with all your heart and with all your soul and with all your mind.'
This is the first and greatest commandment.
And the second is like it: 'Love your neighbor as yourself.'
All the Law and the Prophets hang on these two commandments."
Matthew 22:36-40

Journal: ________________________________

12
Wedding Dress

Paul's Lesson:
I consider that our present sufferings are not worth comparing with the glory that will be revealed in us. For the creation waits in eager expectation for the children of God to be revealed.
Romans 8:18-19

in the weeks leading up to our wedding day, I met with our wedding planner, Beanie Kelly. She was the Children's Minister at our church and volunteered to help coordinate our marriage ceremony. Her humor and friendship was a gift.

We picked the service, the music, the vows, the menu for the luncheon, and on. The youth girls would serve the guests lunch, and the Bistro ladies would decorate the social hall and cook the meal. My nieces and mother would come in two nights before and bake cupcakes for the cupcake tree. Everything was falling into place. Except for one thing—my tattoo.

I gained several tattoos over the years—two on my leg, one on my lower belly, and one on my upper left arm—the only one that required a redo after my second divorce.

I ordered the wedding dress from the manufacturer. The picture in the catalog has not revealed it, but it was clear the tattoo would show through the sheer design of the sleeve. *The three lavender roses inked on left arm may offend the purity of the beautiful white wedding dress,* I thought. I lamented over this for several weeks and had a frantic search for ways to hide this blemish on my wedding day.

An internet search gave me several options. I could use special theater-quality makeup to hide it at the risk of the creamy cover rubbing off on the white sheet fabric. Another choice was to wrap my arm with a cloth, which meant to wrap both arms in similar fashion to make it look less like a bandage and more like a part of the dress. Ugh, I had no answer and was in a panic.

My thoughts raced, *how could I have purchased a dress that didn't cover this up? How am I going to hide this imperfection? There is no way I can let others see this – this mark on my wedding day. There is no solution to this!!* I felt hopeless. I had to hide the tattoo—there was no way around it.

Meeting with Beanie two weeks before the wedding, we went over the final approval of the ceremony and reception. We sat in the church secretary's office and leaned over the details. I confirmed as she read the list while her pen ticked the approval. We finished and sat back in relief.

"What else, Michelle," Beanie inquired. "Any last-minute requests or thoughts?"

"Nothing," I answered as I visualized the list of items in my head.

"Any concerns?" she asked, taking another approach.

"Nope, everything's fine," I responded, trying to reassure her there was nothing left undone.

Beanie had this God-line of communication that gave her insight. She sensed something was bothering me and her line of questioning was not producing what her intuition knew was there.

"Is there something bothering you? Maybe something you don't want to talk about?" she asked, "Anything at all worrying you?"

I sat for a moment thinking of all the time I spent hiding my tattoo. I admitted it.

"Yes," I said. "Yes, I have been trying to figure out how to hide my tattoo. My dress doesn't cover it. I tried wrapping it, bought cover-up makeup, which rubbed off. I don't know what to do about it," I confessed, raising my sleeve to expose the lavender artwork on permanent display.

Beanie said, "Why are you trying to hide it? That is part of you. Do you think God cares about a tattoo on your arm? It's not a matter of how to hide it, it's a matter of you being comfortable with who you are. Let it go, girl. If God doesn't care, why should you?"

Michelle being comfortable with who she is. That was not on our checklist, but I believe it was on God's. Check! In that moment,

Beanie's statement took away all my anxiety about the tattoo. I no longer needed to hide, no longer needed to cover up—God loved me for who I was, tattoos and all.

The tattoo was something from my past and if God didn't care about that, why should I? He loved me unconditionally. I needed to *be comfortable* and let the past go. And so, I did. I thought no more about the tattoo. I had other things to think about.

Four days before the wedding, I put my dress on to show my maid of honor, Elizabeth, the ensemble I had picked out. My veil belonged to a co-worker, Andrea, who volunteered to lend it to as the borrowed piece of attire. The sheer embellished piece looked like it was tailor made to match the dress. It was perfect.

As Elizabeth was inspecting my dress, she pointed out that the length was way too long. I didn't have heels on, so I went back into the closet to find something to increase my height. No better. Not only did the dress needed hemming, but my shoes were cloth wedges—not a good match. I am not a fashion aficionado, so I was open to her advice.

Not only did the dress, but the train needed hemming. I panicked. *It was four days before the wedding*. I had not thought about having the dress altered in the months it hung in my closet. How was this going to happen? I didn't even know where to begin.

Elizabeth chimed in, "I can do it."

"You can hem the dress?" I asked.

"I have been sewing for years," she offered, "I already took Friday off to help you get ready, so I can come over Thursday evening to work on your dress."

I knew she loved to sew and, as part of our gift to her for being my maid of honor, Greg and I purchased a nice sewing machine to give her. This, just a day before. I thought her sewing a hobby and did not understand her extensive talent.

Elizabeth came over on Thursday and worked on the train hem. I stood on a chair and she pinned the right length. The sewing machine sat on my dining room table and she stitched the hem. She was still sewing hours later and the night grew late before she stopped. Elizabeth voiced her doubts on finishing before Saturday.

"Michelle, I am sorry it is taking so long. I don't want to mess this up for you. I need to go home and get sleep. I promise I will be back tomorrow to finish it." I thanked her for all she had done and told her I knew God would help us through this. She packed up and headed home.

Friday came and I went to the church to check in with Beanie and the team of ladies in the kitchen. Everything was falling into place. My nieces, Emma and Diana, my sister Lynn, and my mother had finished the cupcakes the night before. Each tray full of cupcakes was wrapped and in the commercial sized refrigerator. The next morning, each confection would be on display in the cupcake tree.

Elizabeth called me. "Hello Hun," she began, "I called my mother about your dress."

"Oh, did she give you some advice on finishing it?" I asked.

"No, she decided yesterday to fly up here from Miami to surprise us. She is coming with me this evening to help me work on your dress," she explained.

"Oh, my gosh, that's wonderful," I responded with gratefulness. I had not met her mother and knew little about her. Elizabeth revealed a remarkable fact about her mother that showed me God had a plan—even for my dress. Her mother was a professional seamstress and she had decades of experience altering formal dresses and wedding gowns.

That evening, her mother arrived, stern faced and ready to work. I put the dress on and stood like a little girl, arms out, then down, a pull there, tuck here, and pinned in place. Gingerly, I stepped out when the tacking was complete.

"She needs to rest," her mother told Elizabeth, letting me know she was in charge.

"Good idea," Elizabeth chimed in, assuring me they would have the dress done in good time.

"Thank you both. I don't know what I would have done. This is one thing that slipped my mind," I said apologizing.

I laid down, not bothering to change into pajamas in case I needed a final fitting. I stared at the wall and let my eyes close. I imagined what the next day would bring, trusting God's vision would be far beyond my imagination. I drifted in and out of sleep as the sewing machine buzzed in spurts in the next room.

Elizabeth woke me about 2:00 a.m. and said her mother had finished. I slipped out of bed and moved my tired body to the next room. I put the dress on and Elizabeth zipped it. The lace, the fit, the hem, the sleeves, even my triple rose tattoo—the mirror showed it all as flawless.

"Wait," her mother uttered looking at my braided, cloth shoes, "She can't wear those!"

"What, Ma? Those are fine." Elizabeth countered.

"No! She needs proper heels. You two go in the morning and get new shoes," she commanded. "Not those!" she pointed again at my hippy heels.

"Fine, we will," Elizabeth assured her.

I nodded and smiled at Elizabeth. We promised to meet early to go to the nearest shoe store and make a proper purchase. I needed more sleep and so did the two ladies who came to my rescue. I thanked her mother once more. With the work done, Elizabeth headed home with her mother and promised to meet me two hours before the wedding.

I valued the lesson of being comfortable with my past and accepting of who I was becoming. The only one who was condemning me for my past was me. This would be key in the years ahead as I dealt with more issues, changing life dynamics, and the inner turmoil that ensued as God led me through continued healing.

Although this song came out a month after our wedding day, it resonated with me and continues to draw up images of my wedding dress and the perfection God gives us through Christ. *Redeemed* by Big Daddy Weave is still one of my favorite songs. Each time I listen, I find my spirit resting is God's assurance of Grace.

The perfect fit of the dress, was the perfect fit of God's Love. My decision to accept myself, regardless of my past, was powerful. God showed me that through Jesus Christ, I am flawless, loved, accepted, and perfect in His eyes. Is there more work to do? Yes, but God's love for me will never change—Jesus made it unchangeable and eternal.

God gave us the big day.

Road Signs

In this step, Michelle saw all God had done in her life up to that point. She understood more of the *Michelle* God created her to be, holy and without blemish. She rested because her past no longer defined her.

Reflect on how God sees you with no flaw and perfect in His eyes:

How does it make you feel to see yourself as holy and flawless?

When do you need to see this view of yourself the most?

Why do you think God sees you this way?

How can this new perception change how you perceive others?

But now he has reconciled you by Christ's physical body through death to present you holy in his sight, without blemish and free from accusation.
Colossians 1:22

Journal:

13
The Big Day

Paul's Lesson:

Husbands, love your wives, just as Christ loved the church and gave himself up for her to make her holy, cleansing her by the washing with water through the word, and to present her to himself as a radiant church, without stain or wrinkle or any other blemish, but holy and blameless.
Ephesians 5:25-26

March is so fickle in the Mid-Atlantic. One day could be June weather and the next, it could snow like it's January—it's a gamble. We trusted March 17th was God's plan, but thought it unwise to do anything outdoors—just in case. This day, however, every event could have been planned for outside and it would have been perfect—72 degrees and sunny.

I awoke to the notion that by the time I went to sleep again I would have a new name, a new husband, and a fulfilled covenant with God. I was excited, nervous, and ready for the day to begin. With the dress, makeup, hair products, and veil packed in the car, I headed to the shoe store.

Elizabeth and I met in the parking lot of Shoe Carnival and headed in. I found pearl pumps and Elizabeth purchased a cream pair to match her outfit. With her mother's directive fulfilled, we arrived at the church around 9:30 a.m.

The ceremony would begin at 11:00 a.m., so I had an hour and a half to get ready. But first our photographer, Amy, arrived and I gave her a quick tour. The ceremony would take place in the main sanctuary. Inside, the church ladies decorate with beautiful banners and ribbons signaling a wedding would take place that day. The honey wooden pews held white ribbon flowers lining the way up to the altar.

I pointed out the choreographed plan Beanie set in place. Guests would arrive and be seated by Greg's sons and my son. Elizabeth and I would arrive through a side entrance unseen by the guests and groom. Elizabeth would walk the aisle after the list of parents and relatives were seated. I would enter and walk up the aisle alone, but not alone—God was giving me away.

After the ceremony, we would invite the guests to travel the short distance to the social hall for the reception luncheon. A covered walkway between the church and the social hall would make it an easy transition. Elizabeth, Amy, and I walked the path to see what the Bistro team had been up to.

Beautifully decorated tables placed throughout the massive social hall, each setting awaiting its guest. The tower of cupcakes was staged in the center of the room loaded with my nieces' confectionary creations and pastel flowers. It couldn't have been lovelier if a ten-tiered wedding cake were in its place. The room looked like an eloquent banquet awaiting its guests.

The Bistro ladies had been cooking since early morning and the aromas unveiled the delicious menu we confirmed weeks before. Missy's culinary talents were beyond compare and the meal was reminiscent of a top-notch restaurant. Guests certainly would enjoy the roasted vegetables, chicken, and fresh baked breads.

The youth girls, dressed in white shirts and black pants, were sweet sentinels ready to serve our guests. Each volunteered and some would later be in my Sunday School class. We would reminisce over the happenings of the day and laugh at funny, behind-the-scenes stories.

Time was ticking and I needed to go to the second floor of the education building. The upper Sunday School room was set aside for the bride and maid of honor to get ready. My mother and sisters arrived to help. Elizabeth and I took over the nearest ladies' room to do hair and makeup. The dress and veil would go on last. Amy lingered to take candid shots.

Ah, the dress. Hours before, I slipped it on for the final look before draping it in plastic to carry to the church. With my maid of honor, my sisters, mother and the photographer, I felt too exposed to disrobe. I made everyone turn around so I could at least get the dress over my strapless bra.

My mother helped me with the zipper, the veil, and my newly purchased shoes while Amy snapped away for the photo album. Elizabeth's mother was right. The new shoes were a better pairing with the dress than the hippie wedges.

The veil, from Andrea, the co-worker whose wedding was the summer before, was a jewel lined beauty and would act as my *something borrowed*. My great-grandmother's ruby and diamond engagement ring was the *something old*, shoes were *something new*, and a handmade blue garter belt from one lady from work was the *something blue*.

We all moved out into the hallway so we could take group pictures. By that time, Beanie had come up to check on us—more like make sure we were moving along to stay on time. Most weddings start a little late, but I was ready. I didn't want to wait any longer. Amy took a few more photos and Beanie suggested the everyone head down to the church to be seated.

I said, "Wait, let's say a prayer first."

Everyone gathered in a circle and held hands. I gave thanks to God for the day, the friends and family, for my soon to be husband, but most of all for His Son, my Savior. I was truly thankful for His Sacrifice for me, and in Jesus' Name I prayed. A round of Amen and the group traveled down the stairs and out the side door.

Beanie asked, "Are you ready?"

"Yes!" I said "I am so ready for this. Let's go."

Elizabeth and I gathered our homemade bouquets, hers a set of beautiful white flowers complimenting my calla lilies. Both wrapped in white ribbon. We moved carefully down the steps to the first floor and headed across to the side entrance of the church.

Greg's sons and my son were lined up with my sisters, Greg's daughter, and my mother. I walked in to wait in the shadows until each pair entered the church. They turned their heads and looked over. I got thumbs up from Greg's youngest and smiles from all the others. I waved back and gave a silent *thank you*.

The *Hawaiian Wedding* song played as Elizabeth entered the double doorway of the sanctuary. Abi, one of our church members, was running the sound board with our musical choices. He was hidden from view, but knew each moment and cue to start the next song. Beanie could see me and the sanctuary, ready to wave me forward. I waited for her signal.

I heard the rustling of the guests as Pastor David Adkins, our head pastor, signaled everyone to stand. The bride was about to enter and he drew their attention to the back of the church. Beanie paused for a second and then smiled at me. She waved her arm gently forward inviting me to enter the church.

This was it, the celestial point of my journey. The covenant, the white dress, the changes in me over the last two years - this was the real me. The *Michelle* God wanted me to see—pure, holy, loved, and redeemed. My walk down the aisle to my beloved would be a walk to honor and worship my Savior. God was presenting me to Greg and the congregation as His precious child.

I stepped into the sanctuary entrance. I was clothed in righteousness, God walking beside me, gliding my feet to the sweet strings of the wedding song. My salvation slipped over me like the white wedding dress, a perfect fit, tailor made and flawless. God saw me through the eyes of Christ, unveiled, unblemished, whole, healed, and His. God was crazy about me and it showed. I felt it, I walked with the gift of Grace.

I reached the foot of the altar where Greg and his sons were standing and Elizabeth had arrived moments before. Greg's expression was one of awe and he explained later that he was stunned. We stood before our pastor, our guests and family, and before our Savior and God to pledge our vows.

Pastor David gave a short homily and we lit candles signifying two becoming one and the joining with the One. We kneeled and prayed together, inviting our guests to join while we all listened to *Were It Not for Grace* by Larnell Harris. We exchanged the rings and vows and were given permission to kiss, the final seal of promises spoken.

We turned to our guests and family for Pastor David to announce us as a couple and Abi played Greg's pick for the processional song. You would think it would be a spiritual ballad or a hymnal celebration, but no. Greg's choice was *Meet Me Half Way,* by Kenny Loggins. Unexpected and so much fun. We floated down the aisle and out the side door to allow our guests to exit at their leisure.

Amy followed us and she took a few candid photos while describing her plan for staged shots inside and outside the church. After replaying key moments of the ceremony and kisses on the church steps, Greg and I were ready to greet our guests.

We entered the social hall and saw friends and family waiting for us. The youth girls were taking orders and bouncing in and out of the kitchen. Music played in the background. It was a lovely celebration of love and friendship.

Greg and I made our rounds of hellos before sitting down to eat. Speeches were made and Beanie acted as MC and game-show host to do a trivia contest of *Him or Her*. A week earlier, we gave Beanie ten facts about ourselves, five for me, five for Greg, and our guests had to decide which fact was his or hers.

Beanie asked, "Who, in the past, was a certified aerobics instructor?" Pause and silence—then my family chimed in knowing I had never held such credentials, "It was Greg!" Bursts of laughter, with Greg raising his hands in confirmation.

Beanie asked next, "Who has rebuilt a carburetor?" Another pause. Someone guessed from Greg's slew of friends it wasn't him. Yep, it was me. More questions and laughter with a great understanding that Greg and I were more unconventional than most imagined.

The event wound down and we thanked everyone who came to celebrate our wedding day. We paid the photographer and made sure the cupcakes went with guests. Finally, there was nothing left to do but go home and pack for the honeymoon.

After we passed out the list of things the grown kids needed to care for while we were away for the four days, we headed to one of my favorite places in the world, the mountains. We rented a furnished cabin close to hiking trails and restaurants along the Blue Ridge Parkway, but far enough off the road for privacy.

After settling in, we were like two nervous teenagers after the senior prom. All the months we spent getting to know each other spiritually, intellectually, and emotionally, this was a new experience. It was the culmination of all we had done to get to that point—it was the icing on the well-made cake.

The next four days, we rested, hiked, watched movies, cooked, and spent time together celebrating. That's what it was and is—a celebration of our marriage—to this day we use the term *marriage celebration* when speaking of being intimate.

With the honeymoon over, we headed back to what life had in store—and it was a lot! Over the next 18 months, we did not understand how stressful and chaotic life events would become, but we were prepared. We talked and prayed through each event. We sought God's guidance to do what we believed He wanted and we continued to connect, understand, listen, and partner with each other.

Most of all—after everything God led us through from the covenant to the moment we met, the revelations, the engagement, and wedding - we knew the key to everything was to trust in Jesus. We needed to focus on Christ—look to Him for all things, be more like Him in every way, and trust in Him no matter what comes. Seek God first and all else will follow—it truly will.

I could end this book now by saying we lived happily ever after like the fairy tales do, but life is not a fairy tale. Our wedding day and honeymoon - beautiful and perfect - were just the beginning.

All the two years prior and the months Greg and I spent in discovery was the gateway to the great changes yet to come.

Road Signs

Michelle understood this moment in time was God's creation and to appreciate it fully. She knew the stresses would come because of the changes ahead, but she understood Jesus' direction to be in the present moment and not worry about the future.

Recall a beautiful moment in your life you knew was God's creation:

Describe the event or moment.

What did you experience?

How did the moment impact you?

What stressors, if any, kept you from enjoying the present moment?

How do you believe God would have wanted you to experience the moment differently?

"Therefore I tell you, do not worry about your life, what you will eat or drink; or about your body, what you will wear. Is not life more than food, and the body more than clothes? Can any one of you by worrying add a single hour to your life?
Matthew 6:25,27

Journal:

14
Great Change

Paul's Lesson:

Who shall separate us from the love of Christ? Shall trouble or hardship or persecution or famine or nakedness or danger or sword?
Romans 8:35

Greg and I have been married five years as of the writing of this chapter. The challenges began the first day we arrived back from our four-day mountain cabin honeymoon. We oversaw a house full: four adult children all on different paths, one grandchild with two more visiting every other weekend, and two pets, Sandy and Marvin.

Although we spent months fully sharing life in words and moments, it was sharing a life physically in every way after the wedding that challenged us. The first few years might have been too much to bear without the foundation God laid out for us. Without my change and transformation, none of it would have worked. I needed to change, follow, surrender, promise, learn, and heal through Jesus.

Within the first two years of marriage, there were profound life changes with family, health, jobs, and where we lived. Within the first twelve months, all but one of our grown children moved out and onward with their lives. My son and I become estranged. My focus shifted to securing a healthy relationship with my two grandsons and their custodial maternal grandparents.

During this time, I was diagnosed with Rheumatoid Arthritis. I was misdiagnosed with another condition five years prior and had been on medication for nerve pain I should not have taken. After getting on proper medication, I had to come to terms with this chronic condition. It continues to challenge me, but God has led me to great doctors and physical therapists who showed how to manage the disease. It's a work in progress.

In August 2013, we got hit with the biggest change of all. Greg received notice that his job was being eliminated and had to seek employment elsewhere. Remember, we worked for the same company. The morning he found out, he walked up the stairs to my cubicle, white envelope in hand, to tell me the news.

"Can we grab a conference room for a minute?" he asked, leaning over my cubicle wall.

"Sure," I responded and found an empty room in which to have privacy.

We sat facing each other and he waved the white envelope in the air.

"You will never guess what this is," he said.

"I have no idea. What is going on?" I asked.

"I have just been informed my job no longer exists after August 31st," he said with an expression of shock.

"What? When did this happen?" I started to panic.

"Just now, in my boss' office, not ten minutes ago," he informed me of the matter-of-fact conversation that transpired.

I sat back in the conference room chair and put my hands behind my head. *Lord,* I thought, *I know You have this all planned. I need to trust You.*

I leaned forward toward Greg and I said, "God has this. We know He does."

"I know it," Greg responded, "Yes, God has this."

We talked a few more minutes and then returned to work.

Although Greg had a new job within six weeks, the time of not knowing was challenging, especially for him. He was used to taking care of things, being a provider, and to be without, even for a few weeks, was hard. The new job was a pay cut, but the severance package he received would carry us through for a while.

Along with accepting the new job was the willingness to move. At first, the choice was Indiana, but a few days after his interview, the offer changed to Pennsylvania. A relocation package was part of the deal and Greg accepted. Pennsylvania was much closer than Indiana and we could reasonably travel to visit family.

He started the new job in October 2013, six months before the house sold and a full move would happen. We had spent so much time together that time apart was something new and unnerving. Once we discussed our fears and expectations, we began a Bible study together. We ordered two copies of *Life Change for Couples: A Biblical 12-Step Journey for Marriage Enrichment* by James Reeves.

Greg worked during the week in Pennsylvania staying at his one-bedroom temporary apartment. I stayed in Virginia and continued to work and maintain the house. Each of us worked on our chapters separately, then on weekends, he would drive home and we would schedule time together to go through the lesson. We realized no matter how much we thought we knew about each other, there was always more to learn. The small exercise kept us connected and helped us intentionally focus on growing in our faith.

We moved to Pennsylvania in March 2014, two full and event filled years after our marriage. Although Greg had moved several times in his career and lived in four different states, this was my first time outside southern Virginia. I can honestly say I was excited. I had no reservations about the move. I would miss my grandsons, but knowing they could come stay with us periodically gave me peace. We would work out trips to Virginia to visit family and stay in touch.

With the move out of state, I resigned from my job in Virginia, but could work from home until my replacement was found. It took about two months for the company to hire someone. I applied for jobs in the new area and hit dead ends. I searched for positions in the evening after finishing my work day. Each one I applied for either gave me a rejection email or never responded. I was getting worried, but continued to pray about it.

One evening, I gave up. I walked into the living room of the three-bedroom townhouse we were living in until our new house was built. I told Greg it seemed hopeless and I probably wouldn't find a new job any time soon. Unemployment benefits were not a choice since I had lived in Pennsylvania for such a short time and my previous job was in Virginia.

"Let me help you," he offered, holding his hands out for my laptop. I shrugged my shoulders and handed it over.

"Good luck," I quipped in total frustration.

He looked for a few minutes and then said, "What about this one?" He pointed to a job title *Business Writer.*

"I don't qualify for that," I responded.

"Sure, you do," he answered.

I read the description and requirements. *Bachelors in English and writing experience preferred.*

"I don't have the education they are looking for," I answered back.

"Sometimes that doesn't matter. What would it hurt to apply?" He would not let up.

"Alright," I finally relented, "I'll apply for it, but I don't have a shot."

He smiled, "If God wants you to have this job, then you will."

I applied for the job. The manager responded to my resume with an email that closely resembled my own reservations. She thanked me for my application, but admitted she was curious why I was interested in the position. My career profile included no writing experience and I did not have a degree in English.

Each candidate chosen would receive a writing test, but before she sent me one, she wanted to see a sample of my writing. Once she reviewed my samples, she would consider sending me a test before she scheduled interviews.

I responded with an email letting her know my application was a little unconventional for what she was seeking, but I defended the submittal due to my extensive background in business. I explained my experience in writing business reports and analyses. I attached the samples of business writings and hoped for the best. She sent me the test.

I took my time reading through and answering the questions. I submitted the writing test in hopes she would look beyond the educational requirement of an English degree and see me as a contender. I also prayed. *God, if this is the job You have planned for me, please, let this be undeniably a great fit.*

I had to leave for Virginia to train my replacement the following week so I knew an interview before the trip was unlikely. On the Thursday before I was to leave for Richmond, I got the email from Caroline. She asked me to come to an interview with her and her assistant manager at a local Panera the next day.

The job would be half analysis and half writing. My background seemed a perfect fit, but I had to convince them of the same. It also was a work-from-home position, something I had been doing for several months for the job in Virginia. I took a deep breath and emailed to confirm the interview.

I met Caroline and Lori at Panera the next afternoon. I was nervous, but felt an ease as the two ladies and I sat together to start the interview process. It was easy to talk with them both and we laughed and chatted like we were old friends meeting for lunch. By the end of the interview, I felt like I had a real shot. I thanked them for their time and told them how much I enjoyed meeting them.

The following Monday, I drove to Virginia to train my replacement and I received a phone call. It was Caroline. She let me know she had offered me the job and asked if I could I start in two weeks. I agreed right away. This was it, the job was mine and I knew Who set it up for me. With odds against me, I got the job and continue with it today.

This same Caroline, the one who took a leap of faith and hired me, also is the editor of this book. God's plan is far beyond my comprehension - intricate, elaborate, and perfect - and highly unpredictable. I love looking back and seeing His perfection.

The life journey continues for us. We know God is in control of every aspect and we Trust in Jesus for all things. It is a daily surrender to not take control again and we work hard on maintaining our intimacy in marriage - mentally, emotionally, spiritually, and physically.

We know how our story ends, with us living eternally in Heaven with our Savior. All else that happens in-between is part of God's plan, and He will guide us each step of the way.

I pray this book showed you the intimate relationship God offers each of us - we are loved beyond measure even at our very worst;

healing and peace is possible through our Creator's Plan; and salvation is truly knowing Jesus Christ - real, here, and living inside each of us.

I pray my story helps you race after a life of growth, to find the First Love again; heal through deliberate change and strengthen the intimacy of the relationship for which we were created—between you and God through Christ—the partnership in which you were designed to take part.

Regardless of where you may or may not be in your faith walk, I hope you find, through this story or someone else's, that God is ready to show you who He created you to be. He will show His perfect, immense, and unfailing Love through Jesus when you are ready. In that divine moment, God will begin the plan of helping you find your own Damascus—the place of healing, rebirth, and profound change.

Road Signs

The great changes prompted Michelle and Greg to draw on the skills God gave each during their engagement and early marriage. They knew the changes were part of God's grand plan and continued to seek Him in all they did. They committed to connect and grow together in their faith.

Imagine a future time in which something may change in your life.

Write the potential change.

How would you feel about the change?

Who would you reach out to for support during this time?

How do you believe God would guide you to manage the change?

So then, just as you received Christ Jesus as Lord, continue to live your lives in him, rooted and built up in him, strengthened in the faith as you were taught, and overflowing with thankfulness.

For in Christ all the fullness of the Deity lives in bodily form, and in Christ you have been brought to fullness. He is the head over every power and authority.

Colossians 2:6-7,9-10

Journal:

ACKNOWLEDGEMENTS

This is the place to offer thanks to so many who supported the writing of this book. Words fall short to express how grateful and blessed this writing journey has been for me. Those who joined along the way to guide, listen, and encourage are in the paragraphs to follow. For anyone I have forgotten to mention, please forgive me and accept my apologies in advance.

First and most importantly, I thank God for all He has done in my life and for Jesus, my Savior.

I am thankful for my husband Greg Williams. You aim to see me as God sees me, as He directed. Thank you for saying *Yes* when He asked. I am eternally grateful that you love me - the *real* me. I love you, my dearest friend.

My editor, Caroline. I value your insight and guidance in this project. Thank you for giving me a chance and for being part of His plan.

My writer circle of friends, your encouragement and feedback is a gift and I thank you all for the support.

My spiritual guides and friends, especially Paula Geter, Linnie Brown, and Karen Thomas, for encouraging me to seek God first in all matters. For Darlene Stevens and Charlotte Hopkins for loving me through my early mistakes.

My church leadership friends for reading this book and providing constructive and meaningful feedback. Rev. Jim Van Zandt, Rev. Mira Hewlett, Erin Fleet, and Rev. Tereasa McRoberts.

Thanks to Youth Directors, Frank Basil and Erin Fleet for allowing me to share the story with the confirmation classes and youth groups in your charge.

To Tereasa and Keith Jackson for raising our grandsons. Tereasa, your presence in my life is a gift. Thank you for listening to my deepest hurts and greatest joys.

My father, Dorsey Howard, who cheered me on through my transformation through Jesus.

To my mother, Diane Howard, who listened to my hardest realizations with love and kindness.

To my step-mother, Debby Howard, for who you are – my friend and encourager.

To my sisters, Lynn Eggleton, for your feedback on the cover design; and Sheila Brandenburg, for loving Jesus and saying so before I knew Him.

My step-daughter, Madelyn Williams, your determination is a God-gift and inspirational.

Ron Figurski, my father-in-law and friend, for all you do day in and day out living the mission of Jesus' Love, and for reading my blog.

My cousin and genealogy research cohort, David Felter, thank you for your wise and sound advice.

My neighbor and friend, Cynthia Christiansen, thank you for our sessions of morning coffee and contemplative prayer – invaluable during this process.

To Beverly Beers. Your friendship and insight in the early stages of the project was a blessing, and helped me realize books two and three.

To Kim Bradshaw, for being the living example of forgiveness and showing me lost friendships can be found when hearts and minds align.

To our Sunday School class, Pathways, for allowing some of these stories to become part of our lessons. Thanks for keeping the tissues ready when I make myself and the ladies cry. Love you all.
The Women of Faith and Friendship life group, you all inspire me. A special thanks to Sherry Monoski for setting the example of a godly woman in action and helping keep the group fed and loved through the year.

To all the couples who set the example of living God's plan, regardless of what life throws at you - Cheers! Greg and I are privileged to know Frank and Claudine Adams, and Dave and Beth Beaves. Your marriages pursue Christ and you inspire us each time we meet.

To everyone mentioned in the story, thank you for being a part of it. It wouldn't be the same without you. God bless you all.

REFERENCE

[1] Carroll, Lewis, and William Sterling. "Alice's Adventures in Wonderland." Alice's Adventures in Wonderland (1972 Film). 20 Nov. 1972. Television.

[2] responsible. 2017. In en.OxfordDictionaries.com. Retrieved February 17, 2017, from https://en.oxforddictionaries.com/definition/responsible

[3] overly. 2017. In en.OxfordDictionaries.com. Retrieved February 17, 2017, from https://en.oxforddictionaries.com/definition/overly

[4] Chapman, G. (11 April 2017) http://www.5lovelanguages.com/ Moody, LaCroix Design Co.

APPENDIX

MENTAL HEALTH AND ABUSE

Many issues were discussed in Michelle's story. Each one is unique and challenging. Please see the resources below to help take the next step. Getting help is key in healing and becoming a healthier version of you.

- If you are suffering from depression or thoughts of suicide, please call the National Suicide Prevention Lifeline at 1-800-273-8255.
- For those ready to deal with past hurts, abuse, neglect, and damaging relationships, please contact a licensed therapist, Christian counselor, or a local behavioral health unit.
- If you or someone you know is suffering from abuse, sexual or otherwise, report it at once to the local authorities.

SPIRITUAL GROWTH

- Find a local church in which you feel nourished and can grow in spirit. Visit each to discern where God is leading you. A resource to find local churches globally is:

http://www.findachurch.com/a_hme/hme_hme.asp

- There are many online resources to read the Word of God. One of Michelle's favorites is www.biblegateway.com

NATIONAL PARK FOUNDATION

The photo on the front cover is from Cuyahoga National Park taken by James Smith, and used with permission.

Michelle and Greg spend quality time hiking the national parks. Please read more about what the US National Park Service offers and how you can help preserve our national treasures.

https://www.nationalparks.org/ or
https://www.nationalparks.org/explore-parks

National Park Service
1849 C Street NW
Washington, DC 20240 Phone (202) 208-6843

MODERN DAMASCUS

There are places around the world which tie in to the Christian pilgrimage - Jerusalem, Nazareth, Bethlehem, Galilee, Capernaum. and others. Travel to those cities are open. In September 2016, Syrian tourism diminished or halted altogether due to the country's Civil War.

Today, Damascus, Syria is a city riddled with human travesties, war, terrorism, destruction, and heartbreak. Reading the news from this region is gut-wrenching. Families and communities flee from their homes with no time to spare and little to carry - most end up in refugee shelters, inside and outside Syria.

Several organizations fight for basic human rights of these refugees, each to be cared for and exist in peace. One of those organizations in Preemptive Love Coalition. If you would like more information, please visit http://www.preemptivelove.org/

Preemptive Love
1300 Darbyton Drive
Hewitt, TX 76643
Phone (254) 400-2033

Preemptive Love Coalition is a trusted 501(c)(3) non-profit, EIN no. 26-2450109.

Or look online for the current list of organizations helping displaced Syrian refugees:
https://www.charitynavigator.org/index.cfm?bay=content.view&cpid=1523

RESOURCES

Books

The Courage to Heal: A Guide for Women Survivors of Child Sexual Abuse by Ellen Bass and Laura Davis

Setting Boundaries® Series by Allison Bottke

Discerning the Voice of God: How to Recognize When God is Speaking by Priscilla C. Shirer

Life Change for Couples: A Biblical 12-Step Journey for Marriage Enrichment by James Reeves

Covenant Marriage: Building Communication and Intimacy by Gary Chapman

The 5 Love Languages: The Secret to Love that Lasts by Gary Chapman

The Power of a Praying® Wife by Stormie Omartian

The Power of a Praying® Husband by Stormie Omartian

Change Your Habits, Change Your Life: A Proven Plan for Healthy Living by Danna Demetre

The Pursuit of God by A.W. Tozer

Boundaries: When to Say Yes, How to Say No To Take Control of Your Life by Henry Cloud and John Townsend

Life Change for Couples: A Biblical 12-Step Journey for Marriage Enrichment by James Reeves.

Music

You can find music from the book through Spotify under playlist *Finding My Damascus.*

How He Loves by David Crowder Band, Church Music

Whatever You're Doing (Something Heavenly) by Sanctus Real, We Need Each Other

Surrender by Third Day, Move

Beautiful by MercyMe, The Generous Mr. Lovewell

Garden by Matt Maher, Alive Again

Eternal by Sanctus Real, We Need Each Other

Alive Again by Matt Maher, Alive Again

Redeemed by Big Daddy Weave, Love Come To Life: The Redeemed Edition

Were It Not for Grace by Larnelle Harris, First Love

Meet Me Halfway by Kenny Loggins, Back To Avalon

The Hawaiian Wedding Song, Guitar Duo, The First Complete Wedding Music Collection, Vol. 1

ABOUT THE AUTHOR

Michelle Andrea Williams lives in Central Pennsylvania with her dearest friend and husband, Greg. She works for a healthcare analytics company and holds an MBA. She writes in her spare moments.

She likes gardening, reading, writing, eating peppered bacon, researching genealogy, and drinking coffee. She loves her God, Savior, her husband, family, friends, pets, and church.

Michelle volunteers on the Board of Directors for MBS4God along with John Venskus, Kathy Mays, and Josh Sheldon. If you would like more information, please visit:
https://mbs4godblog.wordpress.com/.

Michelle is many things to many people, but most of all, she is a beloved child of God who is forgiven, loved, ever changing and made flawless through Jesus Christ.

Finding My Damascus is her first book.

For more of Michelle's writing, visit her blog:
http://michelleandreawilliams.com